BOBBY FISCHER: FROM CHESS GENIUS TO LEGEND

by

GM Eduard Gufeld
Carlos Almarza-Mato
Mike Morris
GM Wolfgang Unzicker
Gudmundur Thorarinsson
Bragi Kristjánsson
Bob Long

Thinkers Press, Inc.
Davenport, Iowa
2002

Bobby Fischer: from Chess Genius to Legend
First printing: October 2002

ISBN: 0-938650-84-X

Marina Sonkina translated from the Russian Eduard Gufeld's *Bobby Fischer: Legends and the Truth,* published in Kiev, Ukraine at the Health Publishing House. Bob Long edited the manuscript.

DEDICATED TO THE MEMORY OF GRANDMASTER EDUARD GUFELD, WHO
PASSED AWAY TWO DAYS BEFORE HIS BOOK WENT TO THE PRINTER.
EDDIE WAS ONE OF FISCHER'S BIGGEST FANS.

Requests for permissions and republication rights should be addressed in writing to:

Bob Long, Editor-in-Chief
Thinkers' Press, Inc.
P.O. Box 3037
Davenport, IA 52808-3037 USA
e-mail: tpi@chessco.com

CONTENTS

Photos and Illustrations

A special thank you to those mentioned below, both living and
deceased.

Arinbjörn Gudmundsson.
Bob Long: Larsen-Fischer 1971, Reykjavik 1972.
Bragi Kristjánsson: Icelandic views.
Dadi Jónsson.
Hugh Myers: Manhattan Chess Club.
Icelandic Chess Federation.
Johann Thorir Jonsson (publisher of *Skak*).
John Donaldson: secured permissions for various caricatures
plus other photos such as Varna 1962.
Lilija Stein: Fischer & Stein.
Nathan Divinsky: Golombek & Karpov, Fischer with Mrs. Filip
& Mrs. Geller.
Unknowns: Lone Pine and other miscellaneous pictures sub-
mitted to me as candid shots over a long period by readers
of our *Chess Gazette*.

PUBLISHER'S FOREWORD

It's long been Grandmaster Gufeld's contention, and also the contention of others including Garry Kasparov, that inspite of the 1992 match with ex-world champion Boris Spassky, Robert James Fischer should have kept his fame as a "legend" intact and not risked it by playing some good chess and some not-so-good chess in a match that did not befit his former status.

I must confess, at first I didn't agree, now I do. Fischer was out of shape, and he could have maintained Professor Emeritus credentials, but none of that interests Fischer. What we have tried to do in this book is to show you the life of Fischer from which legends are made. You will also get, hopefully, a better understanding of the Fischer of now, his extremism, and the views of many others on a wide variety of "Fischer" topics.

If one has seen or heard various broadcasts by Fischer, they will elicit a number of emotions. Some view his character sympathetically and with sadness, others with disdain, reproof, and a feeling of revulsion. We reiterate, this book is not about the current Fischer. This book targets the Bobby Fischer most of us grew up with, complete with a broad paintbrush of variety including games, quotes, views, photos, and articles.

Fischer has always made fascinating copy. Yet, as an editor, it was often with feelings of frustration and dismay that we put together what we knew with what we were trying to find out.

Many of us wanted Fischer to be a hero in a time when the quality of heroes was descending into the pits. Fischer, in these pages, said he has no heroes. Some took up for him no matter how his behavior was reported. Others, infuriated by his lies and contradictions, ostracized or wrote him out of their chess life forever. Forgiveness can be a difficult thing.

With heartfelt hope and prayer, we hope that someday Fischer will return to the world where most of us live, and leave his fears behind. Then maybe he can embark on a new life of trust and fairness.

Bob Long

5

BOBBY FISCHER: FROM CHESS GENIUS TO LEGEND

by Grandmaster Eduard Gufeld

In the summer of 1978 a tall, elegant man entered one of New York City's cafes. As he ordered lunch his attention was drawn to the table next to his where two customers were playing chess. Having noticed that one of the players had lost a relatively simple game, the man pointed out the loser's error. What he heard in response was not flattering.

"But I am Bobby Fischer," said the man.

The players looked at each other with surprise.

"So what?" declared the younger one. "I, for example, am Jack Robbins; he is Ted Kapelushnik, but nobody makes too much fuss about it."

According to the Jugoslav newspaper *Politika,* this episode happened to the eleventh world chess champion, in his own country, only six years after he had earned chess' highest title. There was a time when Fischer's name was famous all over the United States. The Reykjavik Championship stirred the nationalistic feelings of Americans. In cafes, bars, clubs, city parks and even the streets, hundreds of people discussed the challenges of the intense struggle for the chess crown. A real chess fever broke out. Baseball, boxing and auto racing were overshadowed by chess.

New chess sections popped up in newspapers and magazines. The demand for chess literature and chess paraphernalia grew significantly.

How did it happen then, that a recent American chess idol had fallen from his pedestal? Why did so few people in Fischer's own country remember his victories? There is no easy answer to this question. Such an outcome was determined both by Fischer's character and by the society in which he grew up. The name of the eleventh chess champion became a legend during his lifetime. For a long time tall tales, legends, and gossip surrounded his life.

In this book the author attempts to separate legend from truth, to show the authentic face of a man for whom chess replaced, if not his whole life, at least many aspects of life; the man who once declared: "Chess is life!"

Robert James Fischer was born on March 9, 1943 in Chicago. His father was a biophysicist, his mother, a nurse and teacher. Regina Fischer knew Russian well. Until 1938 she studied in the First Moscow Medical Institute, but then left the country without finishing her studies. Later, she mastered at least six more languages.

Their father left the family when Bobby was two years old. The mother raised the two children alone: Bobby, and her elder daughter Joan. She could hardly make ends meet. This difficult childhood marked the life of the future world chess champion forever.

Fischer's biographer Brad Darrach remembers that as a child Bobby was very fond of cartoons. "The Adventures of Fu Manchu" was popular among his peers at that time. This was a story about a Chinese sorceror who could impose his will on other people. Perhaps some elements of Fischer's later behavior can be explained by the influence of these cartoons.

When he was six years old his sister introduced him to the game of chess. Neither his mother, nor his

Young Bobby at the Manhattan in 1958

1958, Manhattan Chess Club—no fear of cameras

sister, could foresee the role of chess in Fischer's future. Bobby quickly learned the ABCs of chess, and at the age of seven he started studying chess under Carmen Nigro's guidance. A year later he was allowed to visit a chess club twice a week. At the age of 13 Fischer earned the title of National Master. As luck would have it, Fischer's introduction to chess took place at a most favorable time in his life.

Soviet grandmaster, Dr. Nikolai Krogius, (who has a Ph.D. in psychology), believes that the best time to start learning chess is at the age of 7 or 8, when the child is ready for a systematic accumulation of concrete knowledge. According to Krogius, participating in tournaments at this age would be too early. What's needed is short instructional sessions, once or twice a week, and participation in easy games. The age of ten is a possible threshold for participation in competitions. This is exactly how Fischer's chess career developed.

Gaining insights into the mysteries of the game, one step at a time, he demonstrated an understanding of the positional game, and a patience at the board that was rare even in gifted adults. From his very first steps, what distinguished Fischer from others was his amazing business-like style of thinking, the concreteness of his ideas, the seriousness with which he approached the "basics" in chess.

Tall, stooping, with a slightly protruding face, waddling in his worn out sneakers and an old sweater, adolescent Fischer looked like an ugly duckling.

In the year Fischer was born, the

celebrated Alekhine, who never came back to his Russia, was still alive.

Exactly a year before Fischer, the future eleventh World Champion, was born, Capablanca, another chess genius, died in New York.

In 1948 the world learned the name of a new world champion, the famous Grandmaster M. M. Botvinnik, who kept that title, with some interruptions, for the next fifteen years.

Young Fischer was steadily acquiring chess wisdom. Occasionally a loss made him burst into bitter tears. But gradually, he would get fewer opportunities for tears. Already at the age of 13, the 'ugly duckling' won first prize in the U.S. Junior Championship, shared 4th-8th places in the U.S. Open, and 8th-12th places in the same type of tournament in Canada. One could sense his desire to harmonize the combinational and the positional strategies in the way the future champion played. Look how the thirteen year old master won "The Game of the Century" from his more experienced opponent Donald Byrne:

D. Byrne–R. Fischer
New York, 1956
GRÜNFELD DEFENSE D97

1.	Nf3	Nf6
2.	c4	g6
3.	Nc3	Bg7
4.	d4	0-0
5.	Bf4	d5
6.	Qb3?!	

Fischer's opponent, a most experienced international master, and member of the U.S. national team, treats the opening of the game without proper attention. Theory recommends 6. e3, or even better, 6. cxd5 Nxd5 7. Nxd5 Qxd5 8. Bxc7.

6.	...	dxc4
7.	Qxc4	c6
8.	e4	Nbd7
9.	Rd1	Nb6
10.	Qc5?	Bg4
11.	Bg5?	

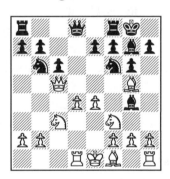

The same incorrect play continues. Instead of developing his pieces, White is trying to create all kinds of complicated situations. The young Fischer understands the situation very well.

| 11. | ... | Na4!! |

An excellent move! Now 12. Nxa4 loses, because of 12... Nxe4 13. Qc1 Qa5† 14. Nc3 Bxf3, and Black has an extra pawn, and a much more advantageous position.

12.	Qa3	Nxc3
13.	bxc3	Nxe4
14.	Bxe7	Qb6
15.	Bc4	

On 15. Bxf8, a very strong continuation was 15… Bxf8 16. Qb3 Nxc3!

| 15. | … | Nxc3! |

Black fires one blow after another: 16. Qxc3 Rfe8, and the Bishop on e7 cannot be saved.

| 16. | Bc5 | Rfe8† |
| 17. | Kf1 | |

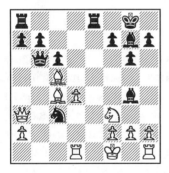

| 17. | … | Be6!! |

After 18.Bxe6, Black would have announced a classical, forced mate: 18… Qb5† 19. Kg1 Ne2† 20. Kf1 Ng3† 21. Kg1 Qf1†! 22. Rxf1 Ne2#. No better is 18. Qxc3 Qxc5 or 18. Bd3 Nb5.

18.	Bxb6	Bxc4†
19.	Kg1	Ne2†
20.	Kf1	Nxd4†
21.	Kg1	Ne2†
22.	Kf1	Nc3†
23.	Kg1	axb6
24.	Qb4	Ra4

The elegant conclusion of a marvelous attack. Now Black has more than enough compensation for the Queen, even moreso, the opponent's h-Rook has not yet been developed.

25. Qxb6

If 25. Qd6, then 25… Nxd1 26. Qxd1 Rxa2 and White loses his Queen.

25.	…	Nxd1
26.	h3	Rxa2
27.	Kh2	Nxf2
28.	Re1	Rxe1
29.	Qd8†	Bf8
30.	Nxe1	Bd5

Eleven moves later, Fischer confidently mated with his great material advantage.

An interesting episode happened a year later when Donald Byrne's brother, and Fischer's close friend, well-known grandmaster Robert, played Bobby at the open tournament in Cleveland.

"When lots brought Fischer and me together in the tournament," Byrne said, "my brother Donald told me: 'Be careful with this young kid, he's an excellent player!' Indeed, the game took an unexpected turn!

"Though I was playing White and had obtained my favorite position in a King's Indian Defense, Bobby attacked like a tiger. Till the very end of the game, I had to defend myself desperately, and after a long struggle, we ended in a draw."

In 1957, the fourteen year old teenager won one event after the other: the U.S. Junior championship, the New Jersey Open, and the U.S. Championship where he got the right to play in the interzonal tournament. When FIDE awarded the fourteen year old Fischer with the title of International Master, he exclaimed with resentment:

"Why couldn't they have awarded me the title of Grandmaster right away?"

The young boy drew the attention of the whole world by his deep knowledge of chess, his sharp style, and his extraordinary talent.

Since childhood Fischer was raised on Soviet chess literature because from 1948 on there were no other world champions in chess except for the Soviets. Fischer dreamt of visiting Russia. As early as the beginning of 1957 a popular Soviet journal, *Chess in the USSR,* wrote about the success of thirteen year old Bobby Fischer, quoting his game with D. Byrne.

"Before leaving for a European international tournament, Fischer expressed his desire to visit the Soviet Union. In the summer of 1958 Bobby and his sister were invited to the Soviet Union where they spent two weeks. During that visit the boy spent almost all of his time at the chess board; he played numerous blitz games, but attempts to organize any serious match with his participation failed–the demands of the young Fischer were unusually ambitious even then."

The "Kid"

In the international tournament in Portoroz, Fischer shared 5th and 6th places, and was awarded the title of International Grandmaster. He was the youngest international grandmaster in the history of chess. He was also a candidate for the title of World Champion.

In March 1980, a Congress of Asian chess administrators and coaches was held in Manila, the capital of the Philippines. Among those invited was the Executive Director of the U.S. Chess Federation, Ed Edmondson. He was the head of that organization since 1970. Talking about his work, he said: "Long before Fischer became the World Champion, we already had a strong organization and considerable financial assets." Then he explained: "Fischer was lucky. He emerged at the right time for that; the U.S. held lots of tournaments using the Swiss system, so he could participate and gain the necessary experience."

Feeling, however, that he somewhat exaggerated his own role in creating a new chess talent, Edmondson added: "Of course, we were lucky too. Fischer turned out to be so talented."

It's hard to say who was more fortunate. One thing was obvious, there was little that was positive in the young man when combined with his fanatical devotion to chess, acquiring some of the major characteristics of the American life style, viz.: praise yourself, promote yourself, be ahead of your opponents, and capitalistic greed. At the age of 14, Fischer wasn't making a living out of chess yet, but he was aware that he could become a professional chess player. Let's make a note of that because in the future Fischer would spare no effort to promote the efforts of chess players.

In 1958 a future international master, Bernard Zuckerman, met the fifteen year old Fischer. By that time Fischer's family had been living in New York for several years. Zuckerman remembers:

"I met Fischer in 1958. He had just become the U.S. Champion. When I saw him at the Marshall Club in Manhattan I invited him to play chess. Bobby measured me from head to toe with his cold eyes, said 'no,' and turned away. Somewhere near the beginning of 1959 he condescended to offer me a game. After that we started to meet at the chessboard regularly. At that time he lived with his mother. His sister Joan had already married. Bobby's mother (she later married an English Literature Professor named Pustan and took his name) always gave me a warm welcome. Talking to me, Regina often complained that her son's passion was all consuming:

"'I was the one who encouraged that passion in him. But now I can see that chess blocks other interests. He doesn't read anything except chess and the endless series of Tarzan and Fu Manchu adventures...'

"His talents," Zuckerman continued, *"were really outstanding: an excellent memory, and an ability to grasp the core of the problem. At that time Fischer was deeply involved in studying Steinitz' work. I remember asking him what he thought about Lasker. 'I don't understand his strategy,' Bobby replied, 'Almost in every game he positions himself badly, but then somehow he manages to win most of them...'*

"I noticed that Fischer got annoyed by everything that he didn't understand, whether in chess or in anything else. And if in chess there was nothing much left beyond his comprehension, his ideas about other things were pretty vague..."

For many years the press wrote about Fischer: "Uneducated type, unenlightened mind, he only has two years of high school under his belt."

When this "uneducated type" beat the 'educated' Grandmasters, some of them with doctorates, the media decided it wasn't such a good idea to mention his high school education and kept silent on the subject.

Early on Fischer's ability to devote himself completely to chess yielded results. At the age of 14 he realized that many subjects in the school curriculum would be of little use to him. As for education...

After all, he "mastered" several languages. That was really important for chess.

Bent Larsen remembers:

"In 1959 I was Fischer's second at the candidates' tournament and I kept saying to

him: 'Bobby, you should finish high school!'

Fischer looking at Gil Ramirez' (glasses) game.

"'What for?' replied the 16 year old Grandmaster. 'They are idiots there, both students and teachers! Only one teacher was not so stupid: he was not a bad chess player...'

"It now seems to me that Fischer regrets that and would really like to fill in the gaps in his education. Because of his outstanding abilities and natural receptivity to knowledge, he achieved some results, but he still feels very insecure in everything unrelated to chess. For example, he used to come to a restaurant with his friends, and if confronted with a weak chess player, he would say: 'Oh no, that's no good,' and would only play with the strongest player.

Fischer would avoid any conversation if the topic was unknown to him. He would talk to his counterpart about the Sicilian Defense instead. Or, say, we are in a Italian restaurant with opera singers performing. Everyone admires the wonderful music and singing, Fischer is the only one who shows no reaction whatsoever. Hiding his face in a chess journal, he is studying some game..."

In December 1958, the U.S. Championship was held at the Manhattan Chess Club in New York. Tall Bobby, and small Samuel Reshevsky, wearing his thick horn-rimmed spectacles, already bald, started the battle after the arbiter Hans Kmoch pushed the button signalling White to begin. [See photo on page 9.]

R. Fischer-S. Reshevsky
U.S. Championship 1958
SICILIAN DEFENSE B35

1.	e4	c5
2.	Nf3	Nc6
3.	d4	cxd4
4.	Nxd4	g6
5.	Be3	Bg7
6.	Nc3	Nf6
7.	Bc4	0-0
8.	Bb3	Na5
9.	e5	Ne8

If only Reshevsky had known the

consequences of this move!

10. Bxf7†!

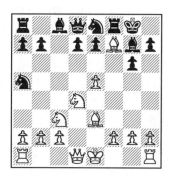

What should Black do? If 10... Rxf7, then 11. Ne6! and the Queen is lost. With 10... Kxf7, then with 11. Ne6! it is bad to take the Knight with the King since the rest for Black is pathetic: 12. Qd5† Kf5 13. g4† Kxg4 14. Rg1† Kh4 15. Qd4† Kh3 16. Qg4 Kxh2 17. Qg3#.

After a long think, however, Reshevsky played

10. ... Kxf7
11. Ne6!

and after 12. Qxd8 he dragged out the defense, but on his 42nd move he finally acknowledged defeat.

This game turned out to be decisive. Fischer finished first, being one point ahead of Reshevsky.

What's interesting is that in the opening, Bobby didn't make a single move of his own; he only repeated the moves of White in one of the games which had been played at a Russian Federation tournament. He knew that game cold!

From childhood Fischer attributed great importance to chess knowledge. He diligently studied the legacies of the old masters, analyzed games and endgames which were published regularly in periodicals. He paid special attention to Soviet chess publications. He was a perfect master of the openings, and the middlegame. He really became a universal chess player: Mar del Plata 1959, third and fourth places; Zürich 1959, third and fourth places; Mar del Plata 1960, first and second places; Reykjavik 1960, first place. Already in the sixties, the Soviet World Champions felt Fischer's panting breath behind their backs. He was second in the 1961 tournament in Bled, and had won a brilliant victory a year later in Stockholm. The endgame with Unzicker shows how Fischer was gradually perfecting his technique.

R. Fischer-W. Unzicker
Zürich 1959

How does one make use of the extra pawn? This is a definite endgame where Black's Knight doesn't seem to be weaker than the Bishop.

Here is how the 16 year old Fischer played.

1. f4!

Another passed pawn is created, and now Black's Knight will be pulled in all directions.

| 1. | ... | Ke7 |
| 2. | Kf3 | Nf6 |

On 2... h5, then 3. Bc4 and if 3... Kd7, White answers with 4. Bf7.

| 3. | Bb5! | Ke6 |
| 4. | Bc4† | Ke7 |

On 4... Kd7? 5. fxe5 and now 5... Nd7 is not possible.

5. c6!

White uses the fact that if 5... Kd6?, then 6. fxe5† Kxe5 7. c7 wins.

5.	...	Ne8
6.	fxe5	h6
7.	Ke3	Nc7
8.	Kd4	

The advantage of the active Bishop over the passive Knight is obvious. There is the threat of the white King marching to b6. Black tried to create his own passed pawn on another file.

| 8. | ... | h5 |
| 9. | Ke3! | |

So, it is possible to come back.

9.	...	g5
10.	Be2!	h4
11.	gxh4	gxh4
12.	Bc4!	

Fischer's Bishop manages to be

everywhere!

12.	...	Ne8
13.	Kf4	Kd8
14.	Kg4	Kc7
15.	Bf7!	Ng7
16.	Kxh4	Kxc6
17.	Kg5	

Black resigned. Black can only save the Knight by moving into a lost pawn endgame: 17... Kd7 18. Kf6 Ne8† 19. Bxe8† Kxe8 20. Ke6.

During October-November 1960, the XIVth Chess Olympics was held in Leipzig. For the first time, the seventeen year old Fischer, the new American star, appeared. He played Board One.

The rest of the team consisted of D. Byrne, Bisguier, Lombardy and reserve chess players, Weinstein and Rossolimo were part of the American team that took second place (first went to the Soviets). The silver medals were the first medals the Americans received in the post-war Olympics. Though Bobby lost to Gligoric, he finished third on Board One (after Robatsch and Tal).

The following games were played by Fischer at the Leipzig Olympics.

R. Fischer-M. Euwe
Leipzig 1960
Caro-Kann Defense B13

In the introduction to this game from Fischer's *My 60 Memorable Games* Larry Evans noted that though ex-world champion Euwe was considered a leading authority on opening theory it was surprising that he chose such a risky line.

Fischer, in an earlier discussion of this line with Pal Benko, had found a subtlety at move 15 which caught the 1935 World Champion offguard. By move 18 the game headed for the ending and was effectively over by move 22.

1.	e4	c6
2.	d4	d5
3.	exd5	cxd5
4.	c4	

Fischer was convinced at that time that the Panov-Botvinnik Attack was the most dangerous continuation for Black to face.

4.	...	Nf6
5.	Nc3	Nc6
6.	Nf3	Bg4
7.	cxd5	Nxd5
8.	Qb3	Bxf3
9.	gxf3	e6
10.	Qxb7	Nxd4
11.	Bb5†	Nxb5
12.	Qc6†	Ke7
13.	Qxb5	Nxc3
14.	bxc3	Qd7
15.	Rb1	Rd8
16.	Be3	Qxb5
17.	Rxb5	Rd7
18.	Ke2	f6
19.	Rd1!	

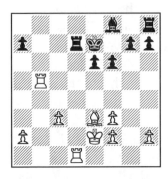

R. Letelier-R. Fischer
Leipzig 1960
KING'S INDIAN DEFENSE E70

Striving to keep a material plus, Letelier breaks opening principles, and ignores the development of his own pieces. He makes the daring move 5. e5 and starts "grabbing." This tactic proves to be risky. Striking blows from the depth of his defense, Fischer destroys the white center. Letelier is not focused on strengthening his flank. He leaves his King in the center. Fischer surrounds the King and through an unexpected Queen sacrifice forces the King to give up.

19.	...	Rxd1
20.	Kxd1	Kd7
21.	Rb8	Kc6
22.	Bxa7	g5
23.	a4	Bg7
24.	Rb6†	Kd5
25.	Rb7	Bf8
26.	Rb8	Bg7
27.	Rb5†	Kc6
28.	Rb6†	Kd5
29.	a5!	f5
30.	Bb8!	Rc8
31.	a6	Rxc3
32.	Rb5†!	

Perfect timing. If 32. a7, then 32... Ra3 33. Rd6† Kc4 34. Rxe6 Bd4 and the outcome is unclear.

32.	...	Kc4
33.	Rb7	Bd4
34.	Rc7†	Kd3
35.	Rxc3†	Kxc3
36.	Be5!	

Fischer does not miss these types of moves. Black resigned.

1	d4	Nf6
2	c4	g6
3	Nc3	Bg7
4	e4	0-0
5	e5?	

Fischer had seen this move in 1957 when he played Andy Schoene in San Francisco.

5	...	Ne8
6	f4	d6
7	Be3	c5!
8	dxc5	Nc6
9	cxd6	exd6
10	Ne4	Bf5
11	Ng3	Be6
12	Nf3	Qc7
13	Qb1	dxe5
14	f5	e4!

The downhill slide.

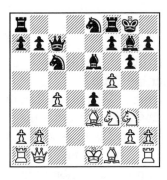

15	fxe6	exf3
16	gxf3	f5!
17	f4	Nf6
18	Be2	Rfe8
19	Kf2	Rxe6
20	Re1	Rae8
21	Bf3	Rxe3!
22	Rxe3	Rxe3
23	Kxe3	Qxf4†!!

White resigned. If 24. Kxf4 then 24… Bh6 is the end.

It was not only his achievements in chess that drew the attention of the public to this young player. The extravagant behavior of the young American grandmaster gave plenty of food for gossip. An unhealthy interest in Fischer's personality was supported by many journalists. I recall the following poem by E. Iluin:

An impossible range of
gossipers begins
from Tokyo to Varnu
All these Bobby-guys are grate-
ful to Bobby that they have some-
body to gossip about…

The Soviet Grandmaster A. Kotov was mislead for a long time in his thinking that "Fischer was influenced by the examples of Reshevsky, and Fine who always bargained for more money."

Bobby learned from his own experience the power the dollar had in his country. The vanity that started to take root in young Fischer was inflamed by his mother. Kotov remembers that when Bobby was 14 years old he received a letter from Regina Fischer. "I would like you to publish a collection of my son's games," her letter said, "Bobby would be happy to have an account in a Russian bank." One of the photographs of the young American champion playing chess in the Central Chess Club in Moscow travelled via the chess press all over the world. That was during Fischer's first and only visit to Moscow in the summer of 1958.

At that time he won many blitz games from master (future grandmaster) E. Vasiukov, and many other masters and even grandmasters. The only player he couldn't beat was Tigran Petrosian who came to the "battle scene" in order to rescue the prestige of Soviet chess. Bobby couldn't defeat Petrosian, nor could he hide his tears after he was beaten by Petrosian.

Time would pass, and Robert Fischer would be very successful in blitz and take his "revenge" on Petrosian. As for now...

In a photograph during that period one can see a slightly stooping teenager in a colorful sweater. On his thin elongated face is the expression of intense effort. He is immersed in the game and does not even notice the camera pointed at him.

After his success in Portoroz, Yugoslavia Bobby finally dropped out of the high school which he had treated with great disdain.

I'd like to digress. In 1988 the *Literaturnay Gazeta* ran an article by Yuri Rost called "Chess: No End to Mystery." The journalist, in an interview with Kasparov, tried to find out if the general education of a chess player normally influences his playing. Would the chess player, considered a genius, be also an extraordinary personality even if he is not a cultured man?

A clipping from an interview with journalist Ralph Ginsberg republished in the British magazine *Chess* illustrates young Fischer's attitude towards education.

Familiarizing oneself with this interview we should remember that the Western media, greedy for sensationalism, has often distorted Bobby's words and actions. That in itself made Fischer reluctant to give any interviews for a long time. So, after having received the title of International Grandmaster, Robert Fischer dropped out of school:

Ginsberg: "And how did your mother look at it?"

Fischer: "We have different attitude towards life. My mother is too stubborn. She kept repeating that I was involved too much in chess, that one cannot make money in chess, that I have to graduate from school and other nonsense like that. My mother wouldn't leave me alone, so I had to get rid of her..."

Ginsberg: "Do you like your school?

Fischer: "I have nothing to learn at school. It's a waste of time. They force you to read books and do homework... Nobody is interested in that. The teachers are stupid. There should be no women teachers, this is wrong. They have no clue how to teach..."

Reading these excerpts it is hard to give up the idea that the journalist trying to take the reader by surprise, and is exaggerating Fischer's words. However, a lot of it is true. Young Fischer removed himself from everything not related to chess. Many journalists used this "weakness" of Fischer's to sharpen their wit at his expense.

Here is an example:

"What do you think about Vasco De Gama?," Fischer was asked.

"What club did he play for?" answered Fischer with a question.

Before the Candidates' Tournament in Curaçao (1962), the 19 year old Fischer was boasting in one of his interviews:

"Mikhail Botvinnik? I'll beat him easily. I can even give him odds. I am already preparing a book about my match with the World Champion. I will win first prize at Curaçao. (In fact, he took 4th place there. EG) [Ed.: See sidebar.]

"What is it you're saying? Nona Gaprindashvili? Is it possible for a woman to play chess well? There is no such woman in the world whom I wouldn't be able to give to give Knight odds before even the game starts and then win..."

The well-known Jugoslavian journalist, Dmitrije Bjelica, who knew Fischer well, and even was friends with him at one point and wrote several books about him, talked about Fischer's not having any sense of humor. But he was quite wrong, just like many others.

Once (this was in 1973), the following conversation happened between Fischer, who was already World Champion, and the correspondent of the *Hollywood Tribune*:

How Did Fischer Fare in His Game With Botvinnik at the Varna 1962 Chess Olympics?

M. Botvinnik-R. Fischer
Grünfeld Defense D98

1. c4 g6 2. d4 Nf6 3. Nc3 d5 4. Nf3 Bg7 5. Qb3 dxc4 6. Qxc4 0-0 7. e4 Bg4 8. Be3 Nfd7 9. Be2 Nc6 10. Rd1 Nb6 11. Qc5 Qd6! 12. h3 Bxf3 13. gxf3 Rfd8 14. d5 Ne5 15. Nb5 Qf6! 16. f4 Ned7 17. e5 Qxf4!

18. Bxf4 Nxc5 19. Nxc7 Rac8 20. d6 exd6 21. exd6 Bxb2 22. 0-0 Nbd7 23. Rd5 b6 24. Bf3 Ne6! 25. Nxe6! fxe6 26. Rd3 Nc5 27. Re3 e5 28. Bxe5 Bxe5 29. Rxe5 Rxd6 30. Re7 Rd7 31. Rxd7 Nxd7 32. Bg4 Rc7 33. Re1 Kf7 34. Kg2 Nc5 35. Re3 Re7 36. Rf3† Kg7 37. Rc3 Re4 38. Bd1 Rd4 39. Bc2 Kf6 40. Kf3 Kg5 41. Kg3 Ne4† 42. Bxe4 Rxe4 43. Ra3 Re7 44. Rf3 Rc7 45. a4 (sealed) Rc5 46. Rf7 Ra5 47. Rxh7! (Geller's move) Rxa4 48. h4† Kf5 49. Rf7† Ke5 50. Rg7 Ra1 51. Kf3 b5? (51... Kd4! unclear) 52. h5! Ra3† 53. Kg2 gxh5 54. Rg5† Kd6 55. Rxb5 h4 56. f4 Kc6 57. Rb8! h3† 58. Kh2 a5 59. f5 Kc7 60. Rb5 Kd6 61. f6 Ke6 62. Rb6† Kf7 63. Ra6 Kg6 64. Rc6 a4 65. Ra6 Kf7 66. Rc6 Rd3 67. Ra6 a3 68. Kg1 Drawn.

"Do you consider another match with Spassky at the higher level as an eventual possibility?" asked the journalist.

"What is an eventual possibility?" asked the World Champion in reply.

Having explained to Fischer what he meant, the correspondent asked him yet another question.

"At one point you have planned a TV series on chess. But, you never got back to this idea. Does that mean that you've given up your plan?"

"On the contrary," said Fischer, "I still consider it to be an eventual possibility, as I did before."

Each year the skill of the future chess champion matured. At the Olympics in Leipzig in 1960 the grown up Robert Fischer was First Board in the finals. He also came first in the U.S. Championship in New York in 1960-1961. In 1961 in the unfinished match with Reshevsky (New York—Los Angeles) the score was 5½—5½.

This match is a curious page in Fischer's biography. The match was organized between the 18 year-old Bobby, who by that time had been a grandmaster for four years, and the talented Sammy Reshevsky, who had beaten many world class masters but who was already over fifty.

The match was sponsored by Jacqueline Piatigorsky, through the American Chess Foundation and the Herman Steiner Chess Club, the wife of well-known cellist Gregor Piatigorsky. The event became infamous, and for a long time was debated in many parts of the world.

During the match there were arguments between the players, partly caused by their religious differences. The prize established by Mrs. Piatigorsky also contributed to the debate. Even the arbiter found himself in the midst of the fight. For example one story goes that on particularly hot days Fischer demanded a fan; but Reshevsky declared that the sound of a fan prevented him from concentrating; Reshevsky wanted air conditioning but Fischer said it was too cold.

Hence, the arbiter, apart from his main responsibilities, also performed "auxiliary" ones such as turning the fan on during Fischer's move, and then switching it off during Reshevsky's.

Fischer himself published a few games from this ill-fated match in *My 60 Memorable Games.*

R. Fischer–S. Reshevsky
New York, 1961
SICILIAN DEFENSE B72
2nd game of the match

Evans said in his intro that the opening was always considered to be Reshevsky's weak spot and he mused as to how high he might have risen were it not for this drawback.

Theory-wise Reshevsky fails but his practical sense helps him to keep afloat, though at the expense of time. Time pressure and Fischer's inexorable persistence forces Black to give up.

1.	e4	c5
2.	Nf3	Nc6
3.	d4	cxd4
4.	Nxd4	g6

Black does allow the Maroczy Bind, but Fischer does not play it.

5.	Nc3	Bg7
6.	Be3	Nf6
7.	Be2	0-0
8.	f4	d6
9.	Nb3	Be6

Fischer said this was an old and second-rate move. Correct was: 9… a5!.

10.	g4	d5
11.	f5	Bc8
12.	exd5	Nb4

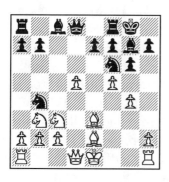

13.	Bf3!	gxf5
14.	a3	fxg4
15.	Bg2!	Na6
16.	Qd3	e6

Fischer said that now Reshevsky started thinking.

17.	0-0-0	Nxd5
18.	h3!	g3
19.	Rhg1	Qd6!
20.	Bxd5	exd5
21.	Nxd5	Kh8
22.	Bf4	Qg6
23.	Qd2	Bxh3

"Reshevsky chopped it off fast— he doesn't wait to be asked twice." (M60MG).

24.	Rxg3	Bg4
25.	Rh1	Rfe8
26.	Ne3	Qe4
27.	Qh2!	Be6
28.	Rxg7!	Kxg7
29.	Qh6†	Kg8
30.	Rg1†	Qg6
31.	Rxg6†	fxg6
32.	Nd4	Rad8
33.	Be5	Rd7
34.	Nxe6	Rxe6
35.	Ng4	Rf7
36.	Qg5	Rf1†
37.	Kd2	h5
38.	Qd8†	

Black resigned.

I must say that in the future the relations between Fischer and Reshevsky, one of America's oldest grandmasters, would not be simple, but rather tense.

Bobby often refused to play in those tournaments as part of the American team if Reshevsky was also invited to play. His opponent did the same. The chess fans were the ones who suffered. The leadership of the American Chess Foundation also found themselves in a predicament.

The 12th match between Fischer and Reshevsky was scheduled for 1:30 p.m. on Sunday. Bobby was preparing for the game when he was suddenly informed that the time had been changed to 11 a.m.

"Why?" Fischer was surprised.

"It was Mrs. Piatigorsky's desire, otherwise she wouldn't be able to make it to her husband's concert."

Fischer replied, "I refuse to play at 11a.m. We had an agreement to play at one o'clock."

"As you wish," dryly responded the voice in the telephone receiver. "Mrs. Piatigorsky will not change her mind." Fischer behaved according to his principles. He did not show up at 11 o'clock and, was declared forfeit, with only 35 percent of the prize fund awarded to him.

Returning to the United States after the end of the interzonal tournament in Stockholm in 1962 (where he came first), Fischer filed suit against Reshevsky and the American Chess Foundation in New York State. According to Fischer "Reshevsky dares to play in differ-

ent tournaments in the U.S., undermining Fischer's authority, since he hasn't finished his match with Fischer..."

The court case was subsequently dropped.

In 1961 Fischer came second in Bled. He also played successfully in many other tournaments. He won a brilliant victory from Petrosian.

R. Fischer-T. Petrosian
Bled, 1961
CARO-KANN DEFENSE B17

This was Fischer's only victory over Petrosian at that time, gained through the imitation of his opponent's style. On move 27 Petrosian offers the draw but Fischer refuses. This refusal may have annoyed Petrosian; Fischer was known to turn down draw offers.

1.	e4	c6
2.	d4	d5
3.	Nc3	dxe4
4.	Nxe4	Nd7
5.	Nf3	Ngf6
6.	Nxf6†	Nxf6
7.	Bc4	Bf5
8.	Qe2	e6
9.	Bg5	Bg4!

Fischer notes in his *My 60 Memorable Games* that "This super-refinement reduces all of White's attacking prospects. Petrosian has a knack of snuffing out such dreams twenty moves before they even enter his opponent's head!"

10.	0-0-0	Be7
11.	h3	Bxf3
12.	Qxf3	Nd5!
13.	Bxe7	Qxe7
14.	Kb1	Rd8
15.	Qe4!	b5!
16.	Bd3	a5
17.	c3	Qd6
18.	g3	b4!
19.	c4	Nf6
20.	Qe5	c5
21.	Qg5	h6!

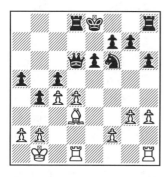

22.	Qxc5	Qxc5
23.	dxc5	Ke7
24.	c6	Rd6
25.	Rhe1	Rxc6
26.	Re5	Ra8
27.	Be4	Rd6?

27... Nxe4=.

28.	Bxa8	Rxd1†
29.	Kc2	Rf1
30.	Rxa5	Rxf2†
31.	Kb3	Rh2
32.	c5	Kd8
33.	Rb5!	Rxh3
34.	Rb8†	Kc7
35.	Rb7†	Kc6

36.	Kc4!	1-0

Fischer had been moving to the top of the chess profession step by step. As we already know, he only took fourth place in Curaçao. But at the Olympics in Varna (1962), Fischer showed the best results on the first board in the preliminary group. A number of successful performances followed: the title of U.S. Champion in 1962/63; first place at the Western Open tournament in Michigan (1963); first place in the New York State Open Championship in the same year, and first place in the U.S. Championship in 1963/64.

In the Varna Olympiad held in Bulgaria, 1962 he plays I. Aloni.

Fischer was maturing. His middlegame was being enriched by new strategies; he won most of his games in the endgame.

In 1965 Bobby played by cable in the Capablanca Memorial held in

25

Fischer and Mrs. Filip, 1962

Havana. Later these tournaments would become traditional. 2nd-4th places in this tournament was a comparative failure for the young American. In that vein Fischer's thoughts about the famous Cuban are of interest. Bernard Zuckerman remembered that after his match in Reykjavik, Bobby asked him: "Do you agree now that I am the most talented player in the history of chess?" When Zuckerman answered that Capablanca at least didn't yield in talent to Fischer, Bobby frowned and began to argue that Capablanca "wasn't that talented," though in fact he valued the great Cuban. When asked in many interviews whom Fischer considered the greatest masters in the history of chess, Fischer answered without hesitation: "Alekhine and Fischer."

In the U.S. Championship of 1965/66 Fischer won again; in the Piatigorsky Cup Tournament of 1966 in Los Angeles he placed sec-

ond; in the Havana Olympics he took silver on Board One. In Santa Monica, of special interest was Fischer's game with Portisch, in which he carried out a very interesting positional idea.

L. Portisch-R. Fischer
Santa-Monica 1966
NIMZO-INDIAN DEFENCE E45

1.	d4	Nf6
2.	c4	e6
3.	Nc3	Bb4
4.	e3	b6
5.	Nge2	Ba6
6.	Ng3	Bxc3†
7.	bxc3	d5
8.	Qf3	0-0
9.	e4	dxe4
10.	Nxe4	Nxe4
11.	Qxe4	

White seemed to get a certain spatial advantage. If 11... Nd7 12. Bd3 Nf6 13. Qh4, White would have good chances on the kingside. Fischer saw further. Black's 11th move is not immediately obvious.

| 11. ... | Qd7!! |

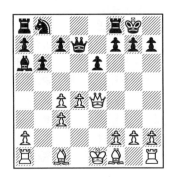

26

Black sacrifices two Rooks for a Queen.

12.	Ba3	Re8
13.	Bd3	f5!
14.	Qxa8	Nc6
15.	Qxe8†	Qxe8
16.	0-0	Na5
17.	Rae1	Bxc4
18.	Bxc4	Nxc4
19.	Bc1	c5
20.	dxc5	bxc5
21.	Bf4	h6!
22.	Re2	g5!
23.	Be5	Qd8
24.	Rfe1	Kf7
25.	h3	f4!
26.	Kh2	a6
27.	Re4	Qd5!

The rest is a question of technique!

28.	h4	Ne3
29.	R1xe3	fxe3
30.	Rxe3	Qxa2
31.	Rf3†	Ke8
32.	Bg7	Qc4
33.	hxg5	hxg5
34.	Rf8†	Kd7
35.	Ra8	Kc6

White resigned.

The next interzonal tournament (1967) took place in the Tunisian city of Sousse. Fischer was reluctant to participate. The official reason: "The prizefund is too small."

Ultimately, he agreed to play. When in the scoretable across from his name there were seven ones and three halves, he left! Fischer's scandalous flee from the tournament caused lots of talk and conjecture. That's why, as a witness, I'll try to reproduce chronologically the events that led to the incident.

Fischer and Mrs. Geller, 1962

Fischer was allowed not to play during his religious holidays. But the holidays, as bad luck would have it, followed one another. As a result, some games were missing in his tournament schedule. So the arbiters compressed Fischer's work week so that he could catch up with the other participants. Fischer was indignant about the additional load and demanded an extra day off. The arbiters naturally refused because the missing games were his fault. Then Bobby appointed his own day off, and did not show up for a game with A. Gipslis. That was declared a loss. When Fischer found out about it he filed a protest. The protest was ignored.

Fischer then left for the capital of

Tunisia, Tunis. A delegation was sent with the idea of persuading Fischer to return. Fischer played Reshevsky and then the question arose about when he could make up the the missed game. The judges said they would not reconsider their decision, and Fischer left for Tunis again. More negotiations, more promises to reconsider the issue of playing V. Hort. At this point Fischer demonstrated his best side. That point is that if a participant of the tournament was to drop out of the event, their results were cancelled. If they played half or more of the games, they would get 'a loss' in all their remaining games.

As we now know, in the first part of the tournament in Sousse, Fischer had to play against the Soviet opponents because of the artificial drawing of lots. He played quite successfully. In the second part of the tournament he was scheduled to meet the Soviets' major opponents, the Yugoslavian chess players. If Fischer had dropped out after his game with Hort, all Soviet participants might have received a decisive score in the struggle for the challengers' cycle. That is why before meeting Hort, Fischer demanded the definite answer to his question: will his game with Giplis take place?

"If I play today, and then drop out of the tournament," declared Fischer, "this would be unfair towards my colleagues. And I do not intend to continue the tournament with a minus."

Fischer liked his milk.

The judges were confronted with a dilemma: to give Fischer a chance to make up for the game he had missed would mean breaking the chess rules. If the game remained unplayed, Fischer would refuse to continue playing in Sousse. As a result, Fischer got a second minus in his tournament schedule and left for Tunis (yet again!)

According to the rules, a chess-player has the right to be absent, for various reasons, for not more than two games. The third absence automatically leads to expulsion from the tournament.

After Hort, Fischer's next opponent was B. Larsen. The game fell on Saturday. On that day Fischer would only play at 6 p.m., one hour later than the beginning of the tournament. This was the time when, according to his religion, Fischer could continue his secular life again. More negotiations. This time even the American ambassador in Tunis got involved in negotiations. They tried to persuade Robert to continue the match with two minuses. The Jury agreed with Larsen to start the match at 7 p.m. so that Fischer had enough time to cover the 150 kilometers that separated the capital from Sousse. The American embassy gave Fischer their fastest car. A helicopter was patrolling the road to ensure "the green light" for the car with Fischer. But at 6 p.m. sharp there was a telephone call from the capital and after that the line between Sousse and Tunis was busy for an hour. At that time I was in a telephone booth, from which Bobby's second, the Yugoslavian journalist D. Bjelica, was conducting negotiations with Bobby. Fischer demanded again that the decisions of the jury should be reconsidered and that he should get the chance to play two games that he had missed. Bjelica left for negotiations with a jury which had again reaffirmed their decision.

I was, at that time, trying to change Fischer's mind, but he kept insisting otherwise. Fischer must have felt subconsciously that he was going to make it for the deadline. Meanwhile, time was passing. Everytime he was on the phone with Sousse his voice would lose its confidence. One could detect the pleading notes in his voice. In ten minutes the chess clock would be started and if the American did not make at least one move during the first hour, he would be scored a loss.

At 7 p.m. Fischer had given up. We heard the voice of a desperate man, who kept repeating into the phone that he agreed to continue the tournament with two minuses, but asked that Larsen wait for him. Everybody rushed to the match committee, hoping they would agree. Their answer: "No, the clock is in motion."

An hour later Fischer was declared lost and for another three years he dropped out of the struggle for the chess crown. At that point Fischer's score was 8½ out of 12 (including the two minuses). Had he continued the tournament I am sure he would have become the challenger.

It is hard to find a man who could love chess more than Fischer. And when asked if he had many friends, Fischer would answer, "Everybody who loves chess."

He was always extremely courteous towards chess. At the chess board Fischer was a gentleman, an exceptionally polite and well-mannered man. He could not stand indecency and lack of respect between chess players.

But, his eccentric, iconoclastic behavior couldn't but create a certain notoriety for him.

However, his eccentricity was only a 'side sauce' to his character. His main characteristic was his boundless love for chess!

"You can expect all kinds of illogical actions from Fischer," Larsen used to say. "There is something undeveloped in him. Sometimes he resembles a big child, very sensitive to unfairness. But he evaluates different life situations only from his own perspective. He is incapable of getting into other people's shoes. His reaction to the world around him can be so inadequate and sometimes so unexpected and sensitive, that relating to him is indeed, very difficult."

After the interzonal tournament Fischer refused to fly in the same plane with Benko because he suspected that the latter had deliberately lost a game to him. An acute sense of dignity and high principles were strangely matched with somewhat childish naïveté.

I will mention several episodes that I personally witnessed.

On the eve of the interzonal tournament in Sousse (the city that Fischer later fled), the Soviet chess players were playing dominoes in one of the hotel's lounges. Suddenly Fischer came up and started watching the game which, as it later turned out, he saw for the first time. He then asked permission to join the game, and, surprisingly, only a few minutes later he was demonstrating a great skill in a game which is not at all simple.

I also remember another episode. A group of grandmasters (including Gligoric, Matanovic and others) decided to go to the Mediterranean beach in one of their days off. I got it into my head to play a prank on Fischer and pre-arranged with the others that I would offer him a tricky problem. While he is thinking, the rest would tell him that the position is very easy and that the answer had been found a long time ago and that he, Bobby is the only one who can't solve the problem! I opened my pocket chess-set and showed Fischer the following:

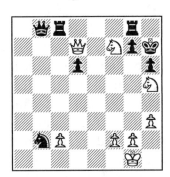

White to Move

"You want some help?"

"No, no!" Fischer shouted. "I will solve it myself!" A minute later the answer, not at all easy, was found.

One should have seen the joy in Fischer's eyes! The solution is: **1. Qf5† g6 2. Qf6** and from the threat **3. Qg7† Rxg7 4. Nf6 mate** there is no defense.

One time Averbakh, Fischer, and myself went to the beach to try our hand at swimming and jumping into the water. It soon became obvious that Averbakh was better at that than the rest of us. However a poisonous fish prevented Averbakh from enjoying his physical superiority. He must have stepped on it while returning to the beach as we were watching him with envy.

The swelling on Averbakh's foot was happening in front of our eyes. That's when everybody saw Fischer in the role of consulting doctor. Either his advice helped, or Averbakh enjoyed quite good health, because shortly he felt much better. During the tournament in Sousse, Bobby and I had frequent conversations, played football, and swam. We discovered that our views on chess had a lot in common.

In 1968 Fischer won the first prize in a small tournament in Vinkovci (Yugoslavia) and in Netanya (Israel), he also came first.

Shortly before the Olympics in Lugano, Bent Larsen and Fischer met in Cøpenhagen. Bobby had shown him a number of games that he played in Yugoslavia in 1968. This is one of the them, annotated by Fischer.

R. Fischer-M. Matanovic
Vinkovci 1968
RUY LOPEZ C92

1.	e4	e5
2.	Nf3	Nc6
3.	Bb5	a6
4.	Ba4	Nf6
5.	0-0	Be7
6.	Re1	b5
7.	Bb3	d6
8.	c3	0-0
9.	h3	Nd7
10.	d4	Bf6
11.	a4	Na5
12.	Bc2	Nb6
13.	b4	Nac4

Obviously this was home preparation, and it is certainly stronger than 13... Nc6, which Matanovic played against Geller in Skopje/Ohrid 1968.

14.	a5	Nd7
15.	Bb3	exd4
16.	cxd4	c5
17.	Bf4	

If White had played 17. bxc5, Black could have responded by taking back with the Knight. Then 18. Bxc4 bxc4 19. e5 dxe5 20. dxc5 e4!.

17.	...	cxb4
18.	Nbd2	d5!
19.	exd5	Nxa5
20.	Bd6	Nxb3
21.	Qxb3	Re8
22.	Bc7	Rxe1†

23. Rxe1

23.	...	Qxc7?
24.	Re8†	Nf8
25.	Qxb4	Be7
26.	Rxe7	Qd8
27.	Ne5	Ng6
28.	Nc6	Qf8
29.	Qc5	a5
30.	Rc7	Qe8
31.	d6	Bd7
32.	Ne7†	Kh8
33.	d5	a4
34.	Nb1	Nf8
35.	Na3	f6
36.	Rb7	Qh5
37.	Nxb5	a3
38.	Nxa3	Qd1†
39.	Kh2	Qd2
40.	Qe3	Qa5
41.	Nc4	Qa6
42.	Qb3	Ba4
43.	Qb4	Nd7
44.	Nb2	

Black resigned.

In October-November the small town of Lugano in the South of Switzerland was selected for the 28th Olympiade. The Americans managed to bring over both Fischer and Reshevsky. They were keen on beating our team, but Fischer didn't like the hall where the tournament was to be held.

"They'll be smoking right over my head," he said. "The facilities are no good for playing chess. If they don't change the conditions, I will not play."

Fischer left Lugano losing a considerable honorarium, but he showed that he would stick to his guns. Subsequent events had proven him right; by the end of the tournament many participants (including the Soviets) complained that the conditions were very poor. In those years chess competitions abroad frequently took place in noisy places clouded with smoke. Today the picture has improved considerably. Do we owe that to Fischer?

In Lugano, where Fischer was replaced by R. Byrne, the American team took fourth place. There is no doubt that if Fischer hadn't left, the Americans would have been higher in the standings.

Having returned to New York, Bobby disguised his location under the nondescript address Box 596.

In 1969 the Yugoslavian grandmaster Kazic found Fischer in the Cardinal Hotel in Palo Alto. He contacted him by phone and then published his conversation with Fischer in the newspaper *Politika:*

Kazic: "What happened to you? You do not participate in tournaments any more, and live like a recluse..."

Fischer: "Yes, it may look that way from the outside. But, my participation in tournaments depends on certain conditions that have to be satisfied. Chess must have an atmosphere for creativity."

Kazic: "Are you playing in the match The U.S.S.R. vs. The Rest Of The World?"

Fischer: "I've just heard about this match. Four games. In my opinion, that is too few. I have to think about it. But I can tell you already that it would be very interesting to play Spassky..."

"To play Spassky..." Robert Fischer had been considering the possibility of playing the Soviet World Champion for a long time.

In this rather curious conversation we have a glimpse of a different Fischer: money was of a lesser importance to him.

I recall one foreign correspondent asking Fischer a tactless question: "Bobby, what's more important for you: chess or money?" Fischer blushed, gave me a look, and didn't respond. Later he said somewhat despondently: hadn't he, Fischer, who knew poverty in his childhood, earned the right to live without worrying about tomorrow?

Fischer's financial demands often made an impression of incredible greed. This was not so. The money didn't really play an important role for him. Before and after the World Championship in Reykjavik, the American grandmaster rejected lots of profitable contracts that many companies offered him in return for the right to use his name in their advertising. He could have easily earned several million dollars.

Fischer was obsessed with the idea of raising the prestige of chess in the world. But, the measurement of prestige in the U.S.A. is money! Hence, Fischer's desire to get the highest possible remuneration for his play. From that came his imposition of higher standards for chess.

On the other hand, Brad Darrach in *Bobby Fischer vs. The Rest of the World,* said that Fischer wanted the kind of money that other stars made, such as Ali.

In 1970 Fischer took part in the chess event of the century: The U.S.S.R. vs. The Rest of the World. The Belgrade chess fans saw a level-headed, obliging, and calm grandmaster. He probably considered his participation as a preparatory step in his struggle for the world title and didn't want to create any problems. That may explain his giving the team leadership to Larsen so quickly and his decision to postpone the dispute with Spassky for some other time. But, Frank Brady in *Profile of a Prodigy,* said that later Fischer regretted his decision to play Petrosian.

All of a sudden Petrosian, who did not expect such a replacement, was faced with an awesome opponent! Fischer's psychological calculation proved right; he won the mini-match 3 to 1. A year later Petrosian wrote with a shade of irony and sadness: "As far back as 1958 I was urgently called up by the Central Chess Club to help cope with a teenager who was beating the Moscow masters. But last year I had 'the pleasure' of losing to him in the 'Match of the Century.' "

Have a look now at the first game during the "Match of the Century." The players were on Board Two.

R. Fischer-T. Petrosian
Belgrade 1970
CARO-KANN DEFENSE B13

1.	e4	c6
2.	d4	d5
3.	exd5	cxd5
4.	Bd3	Nc6
5.	c3	Nf6

Kholmov recommends 5... e5 6. dxe5 Nxe5 7. Bb5† Nc6.

6. Bf4

In response to 6. Bg5, Fischer of-fers an interesting variant: 6... Ne4 7. Bxe4 dxe4 8. d5 Ne5 9. Qa4† Qd7 10. Qxe4 Qf5!?, considering this position fine for Black.

6.	...	Bg4
7.	Qb3	Na5

Easier was 7... Qc8, and if 8. Na3, then a6, obtaining quite a solid position.

8.	Qa4†	Bd7
9.	Qc2	e6

The move 9...a6, planning the maneuver of 10... Bb5, was worth consideration, according to Petrosian.

10.	Nf3	Qb6
11.	a4!	

A timely response. White decisively blocks the maneuver 11... Bb5.

11.	...	Rc8
12.	Nbd2	Nc6
13.	Qb1	Nh5

According to Fischer, it would have been better to play 13... g6.

14.	Be3	h6
15.	Ne5	Nf6

Some commentators have recommended the continuation 15... Nxe5 16. dxe5 Bc5 17. a5 Qc7 18. g4!? Bxe3 19. fxe3 Qxe5 20. gxh5 Qxe3† 21. Be2 Bb5 22. Qd1, and Black doesn't have enough compensation for the piece. In his notes Fischer does not consider 18. g4!?, but rather prefers the positional 18. Nf3, which also promised the advantage to White after 18... Bxe3 19. fxe3 g6 20. 0-0, preparing e3-e4 to try to undermine the center.

16.	h3	Bd6
17.	0-0	Kf8

Quite rightly Fischer believes that the better of two evils would be 17... 0-0, though even after 18. f4 White has a definite advantage.

18.	f4	Be8
19.	Bf2	Qc7
20.	Bh4	Ng8
21.	f5!	

Even though there is a forced exchange of some light pieces, White's attack becomes more intense.

21.	...	Nxe5
22.	dxe5	Bxe5
23.	fxe6	Bf6
24.	exf7	Bxf7
25.	Nf3!	Bxh4
26.	Nxh4	Nf6
27.	Ng6†	Bxg6
28.	Bxg6	Ke7!!

Fischer's award.

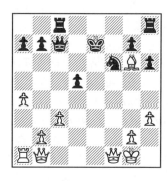

29.	Qf5	Kd8
30.	Rae1	Qc5†
31.	Kh1	Rf8

32. Qe5

Opening up the center, White controls the outcome of the game.

32.	...	Rc7
33.	b4	Qc6
34.	c4	dxc4
35.	Bf5	Rff7
36.	Rd1†	Rfd7
37.	Bxd7	Rxd7
38.	Qb8†	Ke7
39.	Rde1†	

Black resigned. After that match, Petrosian invited Bobby to play in Armenia.

"I would play with pleasure," responded Fischer, "but first send me all the conditions of the tournament. I am particularly interested in the lighting in the room and the list of the participants..."

In an interview with Bjelica, Fischer said:

*"In the U.S.S.R. the grandmasters have good conditions for playing chess. I am a professional chessplayer who has to earn a living by playing chess. If I don't play, I do not receive any money. I am often criticized for asking a special honorarium for participation in the competitions. My answer is: **chess is my life** (bold is mine—EG)."*

"What do you like besides chess?"

"I like music, television. I used to collect suits, but not any more. I have no car, and here in Belgrade, I got a "Moscovich" car, as a prize for the victory on my board. Last year we had 56,000 deaths as a result of car accidents, and I decided I'd rather use buses."

Bobby frequently makes unexpected confessions, such as: "I very much enjoy listening to Radio Moscow. Particularly, the chess editions." At one point Bobby was in one of the largest European museums of Art and Sculpture and was fast with his verdict: "Chess is better anyway."

At the end of the "Match of the Century," all the participants were asked four questions by Bjelica:

1. What does chess mean for you and what attracts you to this game most?

2. How do you estimate the sport and creative results of the matches?

3. What do you consider your best game?

4. What is your opinion about the present rules for the World Championship?

The participants responded to these questions immediately after the end of the event. Here are Bobby Fischer's answers:

1. What attracts me to chess most is travelling, money and the chess atmosphere itself. It's easier for me to earn money by playing chess than by doing anything else. Chess is certainly an art form, but I really didn't give a thought to that. I love chess very much, but I am also interested in many other things: music, sports, politics. Chess professionals can truly live. In no other field could I have achieved such results. I didn't finish school, and I am not sure that was necessary.

For a length of time I didn't participate in tournaments, but chess provides for my life. For the book Bobby Fischer Teaches Chess *I got $10,000. For the collection of* My 60 Memorable Games *I received about half of that price. Also I have a monthly income of about $300 for a chess column in* Boys' Life. *They spread rumors about me that I can't write by myself, that I demand a honorarium for each interview, that I hate photographers, that my demands are unreasonable. This is not so. I work constantly, try to be nice to people. I don't do everything for money, but I earn my bread by playing chess...*

2. The tournament in Europe

is truly an event of the century. I liked the idea of participating in it a lot. The tournament was well-organized and I was completely satisfied with it. We, in the U.S., are lacking such remarkable organizers, the likes you have in Belgrade, who are so devoted to chess. I believe that if you increased the number of chess boards, then the chances for the Rest of the World Team would improve. I did not have time to examine the games of all participants. I am happy with my first two games; in the third one my opening strategy was not good, but Petrosian did not win, in spite of his better position. I intend to go back to participating in tournaments, though I know that much is against me. **I hope to become the World Champion soon** *(bold is mine, EG), because during that tournament I became convinced again that I am a stronger player than the others. I myself gave up the first board to Larsen, because I saw that the team was demoralized. I also assumed that it would be easier for me to play against Petrosian.*

3. My best game so far was with D. Byrne at a New York tournament in 1956.

4. I am content with the system of candidates' matches. But the matches should last longer, let's say until six victories, excluding draws. In matches I am not afraid of anybody. It is a good idea to have the World Championship every two years. Larsen and Korchnoi have the best chances to play Spassky. I would certainly like to get to the point where I could play Spassky but...

As we can see, these are very candid answers and yet at the same time corny, and cunning when he talks about playing Spassky.

1970 was a victorious year for Bobby Fischer. In that year he came first in the international tournament in Zagreb (Yugoslavia) and Buenos Aires (Argentina). At the Olympics in Siegen, Robert played the first board and won the silver medal; in the interzonal championship in Palma de Mallorca he was first again. This is where his direct ascent to chess' Olympus began.

Yes, Robert Fischer confidently moved toward his goal. His real strength was not in an encyclopedic knowledge of chess theory, not in his innovative openings, but in chess practice, in this ability to use all possibilities in the struggle [Ed.: See the article by Carlos Almarza-Mato.] He played each game stretching his powers to the maximum. His credo was: "Chess must be offensive, one should be constantly searching for ways to win. I never try to avoid the struggle, on the contrary, I am always thinking of ways to win."

Although he applied all his mental and emotional powers, Fischer usually avoided time trouble. He tried to spend his time thriftily, and if he couldn't find a brilliant development of the position, he would simply opt for a good move, because he knew many standard games. This was a result of a well-analyzed and developed repertoire of openings, the size of which was constantly increasing. His collection of short games in which he would punish his opponents for faulty opening play is quite extensive. Here is one:

R. Fischer-W. Addison
Palma de Mallorca, 1970
SCANDINAVIAN DEFENSE B01

1.	e4	d5
2.	exd5	Qxd5
3.	Nc3	Qd8
4.	d4	Nf6
5.	Bc4	Bf5
6.	Qf3	Qc8
7.	Bg5	Bxc2
8.	Rc1	Bg6
9.	Nge2	Nbd7
10.	0-0	e6
11.	Bxf6	gxf6
12.	d5	e5

13.	Bb5	Be7
14.	Ng3	a6
15.	Bd3	Qd8
16.	h4	h5
17.	Bf5	Nb6
18.	Nce4	Nxd5
19.	Rfd1	c6
20.	Nc3	Qb6

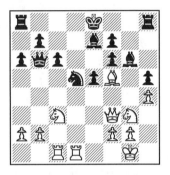

21.	Rxd5	cxd5
22.	Nxd5	Qxb2
23.	Rb1	Qxa2
24.	Rxb7	

Black resigned.

Fischer didn't like blitz chess which, according to him, stifles creative ideas. But, even in blitz he would show excellent results. Always having victory as his goal, he managed to demonstrate theoretical innovations even in speed chess. The following game played in Belgrade is an example.

R. Fischer-M. Matulovic
Herceg Novi Blitz 1970
RUY LOPEZ C63

1.	e4	e5
2.	Nf3	Nc6
3.	Bb5	f5
4.	Nc3	fxe4
5.	Nxe4	d5
6.	Nxe5	dxe4
7.	Nxc6	Qg5
8.	Qe2	Nf6
9.	f4	Qxf4
10.	d4	Qh4†
11.	g3	Qh3
12.	Bg5!	

This marvelous move took Matulovic completely by surprise.

12.	...	a6
13.	Ba4	Bd7
14.	Bxf6	gxf6
15.	Qxe4†	Kf7
16.	Ne5†!	fxe5
17.	Rf1†	Ke7
18.	Bxd7	Kxd7
19.	Rf7†	Ke8
20.	Rxc7	Bd6
21.	Rxb7	Rc8
22.	0-0-0	Qxh2

Small consolation. From this point on the black Queen doesn't participate in the battle, but is only surveying the battlefield.

23.	dxe5	Be7
24.	Rxe7†!	Kxe7
25.	Qb7†	Ke6
26.	Qd7†	Kxe5
27.	Qd5†	Kf6
28.	Rf1†	Kg6
29.	Qe6†	Kg5
30.	Rf5†	Kg4
31.	Rf4†	Kxg3
32.	Qg4#	

In this blitz tournament, which took place immediately after the "U.S.S.R. vs The Rest of the World," Fischer took first place, and ran ahead of M. Tal by 4.5 points. The following story illustrates the fact that Fischer was not deprived of a sense of humor, something considered alien to him.

"Playing with Petrosian," wrote Fischer, "we used to exchange *checks* all the time. He would pronounce this word in Russian, I in English. One time both of us had flags hanging, I suddenly said to him in Russian: 'Check, Grandmaster!' He was so astonished that for awhile he forgot all about his flag and did not meet the time control."

At the Interzonal in Palma de Mallorca I gave Bobby my book *The Sicilian Defence, Dragon Variation.* I wrote this book in collaboration with Efim Lazarev. Fischer, in his turn, presented me with his book *My 60 Memorable Games,*

Grandmaster Efim Geller in Lone Pine, CA

which became an autobiographical rarity. I signed my book and asked Fischer to sign his. He replied, "Tomorrow." Next morning Bobby asked me for another copy of the "Dragon." Soon he returned the book and said with a guilty smile: "Believe me, this autograph will be of more use to you." I opened the book and saw a mini-review of my book on the first page: "To Gufeld. A very interesting book. Bobby Fischer. December 20, 1970."

I am proud that Robert Fischer and I became friends so quickly. It was nice to hear from him ten years later in 1980. He sent his greetings to me through Geller after the tournament in Lone Pine.

We spent a lot of time together in Palma de Mallorca. Bobby often asked me to show him some interesting combinations. Once he pushed me under a staircase to see an interesting combination.

"Why here, of all places?" I asked.

"Because there are no jerks here who could interfere," he said.

Moving ahead of the current event, I will tell you how Maya Chiburdanidze and I played in a tournament in the Yugoslavian city of Vinkovci, where Fischer had played more than ten years earlier. There Fischer met the engineer Angelko Belanch, who now invited Maya and me to visit his house. Belanch knew a lot about Fischer and I asked him to write something about him. He refused. He said he didn't believe he had the right to share the details of Fischer's life without Fischer's permission. To which I responded that if we all had followed this rule, many details of famous people lives' would have remained unknown.

Changing his mind, Belanch then told me how he brought Fischer to a friend of his. This friend had a young son who was very fond of chess. After the meal, the little boy asked the grandmaster to play with him. Robert was embarrassed; not even many adult chess players dared to ask him for a game.

Belanch remembers that on the way home Fischer was unusually silent; he must have had some disturbing thought. Finally he shared it with Angelko. It turned out that all this time he was trying to decide whether he was right in winning all six games against his boy. He confided in Belanch that before the last game he was afraid that losing all six games might kill the boy's interest for chess.

Nevertheless, Fischer won this last game without giving the child the joy of playing to a draw, thus causing the boy to doubt the sincerity of adults.

Every time I read all kinds of media conjectures about this alleged killer behind the chessboard I recall this story, and cannot but stop wondering about Fischer's childlike innocence.

1971 became a year of a triumph in Fischer's life. From the start he beat Taimanov, and then Larsen, with the equally devastating scores of 6-0.

Leaving for remote Vancouver, Canada to play Fischer, the Soviet grandmaster Mark Taimanov made this optimistic statement according to *Russians vs. Fischer*:

"... I can only say that such a chess machine as Fischer has its own weaknesses. Fischer is in his prime. He is now 28 years old... The American grandmaster is a professional, in the highest sense of the word. Fischer is erudite. I know that some people are betting that Fischer will destroy me with an outrageous score. I will do my best to make these bettors go bankrupt!" (Bold is mine—EG)

Alas! The bettors did not go bankrupt!

Many people thought that the Soviet grandmaster could "stop" Bobby, and yet there were quite a few sober voices in this choir. One of them was I. Bondarevsky who estimated that the situation was not favorable to Taimanov:

"One often hears that Fischer lacks the experience of play in matches. But Taimanov has even less of that; he only played one short match with Botvinnik. Fischer is experiencing an upsurge in his creative powers. He knows how to fight in each game from beginning to end, till the game is stripped to lonely Kings on the chessboard, and not many are capable of doing that. There are no tricks in his game, no bluff. He is a player of an absolutely purely classical style."

Let's be honest, Mark Taimanov, who expected that he would meet Fischer eventually, deep down in his soul did not expect to win. He probably dreamt of a draw or maybe allowed for a defeat with a low score. However, his optimism proved to be groundless and he came back to

Russia in a state of shock. And it was not only the score that told about the definite advantage of one of the challengers, the quality of the games spoke for themselves.

In the fourth game of his match with Taimanov, Fischer demonstrated high skills in his handling of the endgame, the delicate subtleties of home analysis. The game was adjourned in the following position:

Fischer-Taimanov

4th game, 1971

Fischer correctly evaluated the game, having taken the game to an few pieces ending.

42.	Ke2	Kd8
43.	Rd3!	

Black gets into *zugzwang,* White sacrifices his Bishop in an exchange for 3 pawns that decide the outcome of the game.

43.	...	Kc7
44.	Rxd6	Kxd6
45.	Kd3	Ne7
46.	Be8	Kd5
47.	Bf7†	Kd6

48.	Kc4	Kc6
49.	Be8†	Kb7
50.	Kb5	Nc8

Not 51. Bxg6? because of 51... Nd6#.

51.	Bc6†	Kc7
52.	Bd5	Ne7
53.	Bf7	Kb7
54.	Bb3	Ka7
55.	Bd1	Kb7
56.	Bf3†	Kc7
57.	Ka6	Ng8
58.	Bd5	Ne7
59.	Bc4	Kc6
60.	Bf7!	Kc7
61.	Be8	Kd8
62.	Bxg6!	

Having calculated the consequences perfectly, Fischer gives up his Bishop.

62.	...	Nxg6
63.	Kxb6	Kd7
64.	Kxc5	Ne7
65.	b4!	axb4
66.	cxb4	Nc8
67.	a5	Nd6
68.	b5	Ne4†
69.	Kb6	Kc8
70.	Kc6	Kb8
71.	b6	

Black resigned.

In other candidates' matches there were no surprises: Larsen won from Uhlmann (5½—3½). Korchnoi won from Geller (5½—2½), but Petrosian had a difficult victory over the young and talented Hübner

Viktor "the Terrible" Korchnoi

(4.0—3.0).

The semi-final match between Fischer and Larsen stirred great interest in the chess world. Bent Larsen dreamt of winning the chess crown from Boris Spassky. And though Spassky considered the Danish Grandmaster the most unpleasant opponent for Bobby, Fischer defeated him with the same score as he had defeated Taimanov, 6-0!

It is worth noticing an interesting detail: in April 1970, when in Belgrade after the end of the "Match of the Century," Bobby gave an interview to a correspondent of the Soviet chess magazine *64*. When asked who had the best chances of playing the next match for the World Championship with Spassky, he replied cautiously: Korchnoi and Larsen. And then:

Correspondent: What match would be the most interesting for the chess world?

Fischer: "Most likely, Larsen-Fischer."

Correspondent: "And who do you think would win?"

Fischer: "I think it would be me."

Before his match with Fischer, Larsen said that he was going to excite the Danish chess public with some surprises in the early games of the match.

"It's going to be hard work, but I already feel myself capable of beating any chess player," he claimed.

Larsen didn't succeed in pleasing his countrymen either in the first game, or in any of the later ones.

The first game of the Larsen-Fischer match was the most creative. Specialists suggest studying Fischer's style by examining this game.

German GM Robert Hübner

43

R. Fischer-Bent Larsen
Denver 1971
FRENCH DEFENSE C19

1.	e4	e6
2.	d4	d5
3.	Nc3	Bb4
4.	e5	Ne7
5.	a3	Bxc3†
6.	bxc3	c5
7.	a4	Nbc6
8.	Nf3	Bd7
9.	Bd3	Qc7
10.	0-0	c4
11.	Be2	f6
12.	Re1!	Ng6
13.	Ba3!	fxe5
14.	dxe5	Nxce5
15.	Nxe5	Nxe5
16.	Qd4!	Ng6
17.	Bh5	Kf7
18.	f4	Rhe8!
19.	f5	exf5
20.	Qxd5†	Kf6

21.	Bf3	Ne5
22.	Qd4	Kg6
23.	Rxe5	Qxe5

24.	Qxd7	Rad8
25.	Qxb7	Qe3†
26.	Kf1	Rd2
27.	Qc6†	Re6
28.	Bc5	Rf2†

29.	Kg1	Rxg2†
30.	Kxg2	Qd2†
31.	Kh1	Rxc6
32.	Bxc6	Qxc3
33.	Rg1†	Kf6
34.	Bxa7	g5
35.	Bb6	Qxc2
36.	a5	Qb2
37.	Bd8†	Ke6
38.	a6	Qa3
39.	Bb7	Qc5
40.	Rb1	c3
41.	Bb6	1-0

No matter how spectacular his play, many asked how did Fischer manage to win by a score of 6-0 in the two candidates' matches against such GM's as Taimanov and Larsen. Let's not bring in hypnosis. This is one of the bad devices that the philistines use in order to explain the failure of their idols. But, the mutual psychological pressure that the opponents exert on each other during the game is indisputable. More than that, inevitable. Imagine the tournament or the match game. There is an opponent in front of you. He oppresses you with his determination, the tension of his posture, his burning gaze, and finally, with his past exploits. In other words, using everything that an outstanding personality has to express his power. You become nervous and you make a mistake.

In 1972, before the match for the world championship, Spassky vs. Fischer, a book on Fischer was published in the U.S. Numerous photographs showed the American as he was growing up. How he had changed over a period of 15 years!

The first photograph is of Bobby, a slim little boy leaning over the chessboard. A timid glance, anxious expectations.

Flipping through old photographs of the future champion we also see a rather lanky man with a stubborn face; then a slim young man, somewhat overwhelmed by sudden failures; a man with a strong chin, and, finally, a challenger for the title of World Champion. A self-assured posture, a carelessly tied tie, a wide smile exposing large white teeth, harsh features, and the burning eyes of a chess fanatic, staring right into the camera. Try, if you will, to play chess against that!

Larsen discards the psychological issues. He said: "I have met Fischer over the chessboard many times and I lost in the Denver match to him. I was not under his influence. The only thing I could complain about was the hot weather. But I believe, so far, the weather does not depend on Fischer."

However, look at this excerpt from the second game of the match; the optimism (or irony?) of the Danish player does not look very convincing. The heat is the heat, but Fischer...

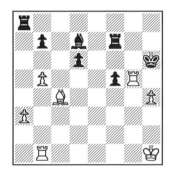

Larsen-Fischer
Game 2, 1971

37. ... Ra4!

Larsen was so unprepared for this move, that further on, he showed almost no resistance.

38. Rc1?

Instead of a possible 38. Rb4 Rxb4 39. axb4 Re7 40. Bd5 Re5 41. Bf7. However, in this case, after 41... Bxb5 42. Rg6† Kh5! 43.

Rxd6† Kxh4 things do not look good for White.

38.	...	Bxb5
39.	Bxf7	Rxh4†
40.	Kg2	Kxg5
41.	Bd5	Ba6
42.	Rd1	Ra4
43.	Bf3	Rxa3
44.	Rxd6	Ra2†

Here White could have quit, but he holds out until the 54th move.

The Soviet Master Alatortzev called the defeat of the Danish Grandmaster in the 1971 match, "Larsen's psychological collapse."

What about Larsen himself? After his defeat he wrote:

"We all smarten up afterwards. Now I understand how reckless I was, having agreed to play in the U.S. Who would have thought that Denver would experience the worst heat wave in years? "The daytime temperature went up to 25-38 ºC and the air was extremely dry – the humidity often was below 10 percent. Because of this dryness I couldn't sleep well...

After the 4th game I went to the doctor who, as I expected, discovered that I had high blood pressure..."

As you can see, Larsen mentions all kinds of excuses except an acknowledgement of his own helplessness in the face of Fischer.

These statements about the match with Fischer were published by Larsen in the September issue (1971) of *Skakbladet*. The article was lacking self-criticism, though apparently the fact that the Dane didn't feel well that day affected his play.

The final candidates' match was in Buenos Aires: T. Petrosian—R. Fischer took place September-October 1971 in the "San Martin" municipal theater. Before the beginning of the match, their total score was equal according to the chess statisticians: 3 victories, 3 defeats, 12 draws. But, Fischer was on the rise, and was younger too. However, Petrosian still remembered the pleasant weight of the chess crown.

Larsen-Fischer, Denver 1971

Do we need to mention with what excitement the chess fans around the world watched the battles between the contenders for the world title of champion? This time ex-World Champion Tigran Petrosian was not facing a 15 year old teenager playing blitz games in the Moscow Central Chess Club on Gogol Boulevard; nor was it the Bobby Fischer who won two games and brought the remaining two to draws in "The U.S.S.R. vs The Rest of the World."

Petrosian was confronted by the leading Western player who was on the brink of his best achievement; by the man who entered the last stage of the struggle for the chess crown that until then had been in the possession of Soviet chess players for more than two decades.

After the sixth game of this dramatic match, the Soviet grandmaster couldn't carry on with full steam. Later Petrosian wrote in *Russians vs. Fischer:*

"After the sixth game Fischer really did become a genius; I, on the other hand, either had a breakdown, or was tired, or something else happened, but the last three games games were no longer chess..."

The result: the American grandmaster Robert Fischer defeated Tigran Petrosian, by the score 6½-2½.

Spassky once quipped: "Looking ahead, towards 1972, I would like to play Fischer..." Now his wish had come true.

Here is the ill-fated sixth game. On seeing it many grandmasters came to the conclusion that Petrosian had no intention of fighting. Or, maybe he was just unable to?

T. Petrosian-R. Fischer
Buenos Aires, 1971
BENONI DEFENSE A06

1.	**Nf3**	c5
2.	**b3**	d5
3.	**Bb2?**	

Grandmaster A. Nimzovich, who frequently used this opening, continued 3. e3, after which Black cannot create the pawn center. 3... f6? 4. d4!.

3.	...	f6!
4.	**c4**	d4
5.	**d3**	e5
6.	**e3**	Ne7
7.	**Be2**	Nec6
8.	**Nbd2**	Be7
9.	**0-0**	0-0
10.	**e4**	a6
11.	**Ne1**	b5
12.	**Bg4**	Bxg4
13.	**Qxg4**	Qc8
14.	**Qe2**	

In the case of a Queen exchange White's prospects look gloomy, Black has an advantage in space.

14.	...	Nd7
15.	**Nc2?**	

Much better is 15. g3 with the further 16. Kg2. Petrosian now goes on the defensive.

15.	...	Rb8
16.	Rfc1	Qe8
17.	Ba3	Bd6
18.	Ne1	g6

White is completely paralyzed. At the same time Fischer unhurriedly strengthens his position, preparing for a massive attack over all the squares of the board.

19.	cxb5	axb5
20.	Bb2	Nb6
21.	Nef3	Ra8
22.	a3	Na5

The better move was 22... Rf7, moving the Rook to the queenside.

23.	Qd1	Qf7
24.	a4	bxa4
25.	bxa4	c4?!

25... Rfc8 was stronger.

26.	dxc4	Nbxc4
27.	Nxc4	Nxc4
28.	Qe2	Nxb2

Fischer heads for the endgame, which can hardly be considered profitable for Black, but the main features lie ahead.

29.	Qxb2	Rfb8
30.	Qa2	Bb4
31.	Qxf7†	Kxf7
32.	Rc7†	Ke6
33.	g4	Bc3
34.	Ra2	Rc8
35.	Rxc8	Rxc8
36.	a5	Ra8
37.	a6	Ra7
38.	Kf1	g5

An important move. Otherwise, if the King goes to the queenside,

g4-g5 will follow.

39.	Ke2	Kd6
40.	Kd3	Kc5
41.	Ng1	

White has no time for 41. h4. Black can respond with 41... gxh4 42. Nxh4 Kb4 43. Nf3 Kb3, winning the a-pawn.

41.	...	Kb5

In this position the game was adjourned.

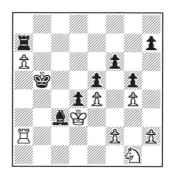

42.	Ne2	

The sealed move.

42.	...	Ba5
43.	Rb2†	Kxa6
44.	Rb1	Rc7
45.	Rb2	Be1
46.	f3	

46. Rb1 looked much better. If now 46... Bxf2, then 47. Rf1 Be3 48. Rxf6† Kb5 49. Re6 Ra7 50. Rxe5† Kb4 51. Nxd4 Ra3† 52. Ke2 Bxd4 53. Rxg5. This position apparently is drawn.

46.	...	Ka5
47.	Rc2	Rb7
48.	Ra2†	Kb5
49.	Rb2†	Bb4

50.	Ra2	Rc7
51.	Ra1	Rc8
52.	Ra7?	

A wrong move, caused by an ill-conceived strategy. 52. Ra2 was better.

52.	...	Ba5
53.	Rd7	Bb6

If 53. Rxh7, the same answer of 53... Bb6 would have followed.

54.	Rd5†	Bc5
55.	Nc1	Ka4
56.	Rd7	Bb4
57.	Ne2	Kb3
58.	Rb7	Ra8
59.	Rxh7	Ra1
60.	Nxd4†	exd4
61.	Kxd4	Rd1†
62.	Ke3	Bc5†
63.	Ke2	Rh1
64.	h4	Kc4
65.	h5	Rh2†
66.	Ke1	Kd3

White resigned.

Having won this game, Fischer felt very confident; he was now sure he would win the whole match. He even talked to the journalists, though previously in Buenos Aires, he didn't welcome them. It was then that the weather in Argentina got really bad; it was raining all the time. Both opponents were afraid to catch a cold and tried to stay inside as much as possible. As they went up onto the stage where they were supposed to play, their jackets were soaked. This led to a joke in one Argentinian newspaper: "Now with Petrosian falling behind his opponent by 2 points, he will have to take off his jacket and roll up his sleeves both literally and metaphorically..."

Alas! Even if Tigran Petrosian did roll up his sleeves, different from the way Taimanov and Larsen did before him, he was unable to stop Fischer's lunge toward the chess crown.

If people quickly came to terms with the defeat of Taimanov (with a crushing score), after Larsen's and Petrosian's collapse it became clear: no amount of excuses from the defeated can overrun the power of the future champion. These "matches showed that Fischer was true to his chess beliefs. He sticks to the classical style of playing, his moves are seemingly simple, but sharp and refined, he calculates all the variants quickly and easily." (M. Beilin)

Chess players know only too well the history of the battle between Spassky and Fischer. Yet, I will refresh the reader about some of the details.

Some headlines might ask: Who will win the coming match? Will Boris Spassky be able to defend his title as the world's strongest chess player?

"The match between Bobby Fischer and Boris Spassky will be the most outstanding event since the times of Alekhine–Capablanca in 1927," wrote the chess reporter for the magazine *America*, Edward Albee.

Opinions were divided. Some of the specialists preferred Spassky. However, in a big choir of future foretellers, there were 'soloists' who didn't doubt (much as the American contender himself didn't doubt) Bobby Fischer's victory. I remember M. Beilin writing in the biweekly *64*: "Before the battle in Sousse I had a chance to write: 'By that time (1972), Fischer would have been 29 years old. 14 years of grandmaster experience. Could Fischer be planning his major battle for 1972?"

From the very first days after the end of the match with Petrosian and while FIDE was fighting with the American grandmaster before his meeting with Spassky in Reykjavik, Robert Fischer was preparing for the final match with an energy, perseverance and concentration worthy of emulation.

"The training process of the 29 year old contender," said the weekly *Za Rubezhom* of April 1972, "consisted of studying the Wildhagen red book of Spassky's games that Fischer carries with him even into the canteen. Usually he eats alone, either reading a book, or playing chess on his pocket-size chess set."

Up to the very last minute, Bobby wouldn't agree to play in Reykjavik. Finally, on May 6, 1972 FIDE received a telegram from Fischer, signed by Edmondson and Marshall. "Bobby Fischer agrees to play in Iceland at the appointed time, but he expresses a protest."

Bobby's further actions were erratic. I believe they had been planned beforehand with the goal of creating havoc. In his book *Bobby Fischer Versus the Rest of the World*, Fischer's biographer Brad Darrach describes Bobby's behavior before his match with Spassky and about his impending arrival in Iceland. No one seemed certain when he would arrive:

"Monday June 26 I called Bobby myself. 'Hi, Brad! How ya doin'?' The words were Bobby but the voice was startingly confident. I had expected what I usually heard when Bobby picked up the phone, a faint suspicious 'uuuuh?...' Then he wanted to know how Spassky looked. 'Nervous.' I told him, and he guffawed. 'And Geller?' I intended to say something about Yefim Geller, Spassky's second. 'Geller is stupid!'..."Geller is stupid." [Ed.: female Icelandic telephone operator trying to mimic Fischer's Brooklyn accent.] *Bobby gasped. 'They're listen-*

ing in on my phone calls!' he yelled... 'Imagine that! Listening in on my phone calls! It could be the Russians, y' know? They' ll do anything to find out what I' m thinking!' "

Fischer's biographer doesn't explain these psychological quirks and "erratic" behavior. In Darrach's book Fischer's state of mind on the eve of the match with Spassky is described with great detail. All this helps to understand why three years later the American grandmaster refused to play with Anatoly Karpov.

It was June 29, Thursday morning, three days before the first game of the tournament with Boris Spassky for the world chess title. There was a knock at the door, it was repeated again. Who could it be? Only his lawyer and a couple of close friends knew that he has stayed at the "Yale Club."

"Package for Mr. Fischer," Darrach reported.

Reluctantly, the semi-dozing Bobby opened the door slightly, figuring to see "Club" personnel. Instead, there was a short, stocky man in street clothes. The stranger blocked the door with his foot.

"Excuse me, Mr. Fischer, but I wonder if..." said the stranger with undue familiarity, said Darrach. Further, Fischer asked, "Who are you?" in a panicky state. He was a British journalist who wanted to interview Bobby.

In the next moment he was calling Andrew Davis, one of his lawyers. Darrach wrote that Davis said, "Don't leave the room. Someone will come to you as quickly as possible."

Harold Schonberg, a *New York Times* correspondent wrote:

"Fischer obtains full confidence in himself and plays at his best only when he manages to bring everybody into a state of nervous expectation; when the organizers, spectators, a judge and his opponent obey his every whim..."

To which Larsen later remarked:

"Many consider Fischer to be a 'big child' and in some way, that is true. But let's not forget that sometimes children can be very cunning and manage to impose their will on those around them... Remember how Fischer managed to convince so many people that he was the 'uncrowned' World Champion long before the really earned the title? Or take his ability to impose his own will on his opponents. Both I, after Denver, and Petrosian, after Buenos Aires, have

warned that one should not make concessions to Fischer; and yet in Reykjavik, Spassky obediently carried out Fischer's will several times... The aura of exclusiveness is indispensable for Fischer. This helps him to combat his constant fits of uncertainty. He only is able to overcome that feeling when he manages to feel the psychological weakness in his opponent."

That was a very true observation. At the appointed time, Fischer failed to arrive for the drawing of lots, and by July 2 he hadn't shown up for the game. However, Dr. Euwe, then the President of the International Chess Federation (FIDE) delayed the match for two more days saying that allegedly Bobby notified FIDE about his illness.

In spite of that, on July 1, there was the official opening of the Spassky–Fischer match in Reykjavik, but it happened without a challenger. All newspapers were asking the same question: "Where is Fischer?" And this is where the Soviet delegation, as well as Spassky himself, had yielded to the will of the American grandmaster, exactly in keeping with what Larsen said:

"At one of the press confer-

ences, Spassky's second, Geller, said that the situation created by Fischer was unprecedented in the history of chess. 'This incident is enough for Boris Spassky to stop all the negotiations and return home. The only thing that was keeping Spassky from this step, is the understanding of the meaning of chess for the world of chess and hospitable Iceland.'"

That was the first concession to Fischer. However, it allowed him to dictate his conditions. The rules of FIDE did not foresee, at all, the absence of one of the participants from the opening of the tournament. However, this is exactly what happened.

Boris Spassky filed a complaint about breaking the rules of the match. The match hadn't started either on the 5th, or on the 6th of July. Surrounded by attention and empathy, Boris Spassky was patiently waiting for the challenger, staying in the "Saga" hotel, one of the best in the city. It was only on July 4th that Fischer finally arrived at Keflavik Airport, an American military base not far from Reykjavik. He must have realized that he could not procrastinate any longer. The journalists were not allowed to approach the plane while Fischer, escorted by the police, was disembarking. The grandmaster stayed in a private home, paid a visit out of politeness to the organizers of the tournament, to Max Euwe and, finally, to his opponent, Boris Spassky.

On July 6, there were the drawing of lots, conducted by the main arbiter, Lothar Schmid. On behalf of FIDE, the Englishman Harry Golombek declared that the first game would take place on July 11th. The World Champion played his first game with the white pieces.

Fischer lost the first game. There were many reasons for that, not the least of which was pre-game anxiety which, one should pay Fischer his due, he overcame quite quickly.

"It is a miracle that he was behind the chessboard at all in Reykjavik," said American grandmaster Lombardy two years later. "I'm not at all sure that this miracle will ever be repeated."

Fischer didn't show up for the second game and a zero was recorded. He won the third game. In game four Spassky probably missed a win. Spassky also made a gross mistake in the fifth game. The sixth game, in my opinion, was the pivotal point. This is the story.

Several months before the described events, a chess tournament devoted to the Armed Forces was played in Moscow. In one of the Bondarevsky–Makagonov System lines, Geller was defeated by Fur-man. On that day Boris Spassky arrived to watch the matches. Four of us, Spassky, Geller, Furman and I, spent a lot of time analyzing this position ... and we found a very elegant and interesting reinforcement of the position.

As fate would have it, in the sixth game Fischer-Spassky, exactly the same position occurred again. When I familiarized myself with the text of the game, I discovered to my amazement that Boris had not chosen the most powerful continuation. Could he have forgotten it? The only explanation is psychological. Psychological factors in general played a great role in this match. [The new find made its way to the chess world, however. In 1973 at the AVRO tournament in Holland, grandmaster Geller, in Timann-Geller, made the move "forgotten" by Spassky. The *Chess Informant* singled out this game as the best creative achievement of the second half of 1973 and awarded it first place.] Here is the famous sixth game, a turning point in the match:

R. Fischer-B. Spassky
Reykjavik 1972
Queen's Gambit D59

1. c4   e6

The system of defense that Spassky chose for this match could not have been unexpected by Fischer.

Spassky had used the same system in two world championship matches. And Fischer knew, after he made the move 1... e6, that he could use the Tartakover—Bondarevsky–Makagonov Variation .

2.	Nf3	d5
3.	d4	Nf6
4.	Nc3	Be7
5.	Bg5	0-0
6.	e3	h6
7.	Bh4	b6
8.	cxd5	Nxd5
9.	Bxe7	Qxe7
10.	Nxd5	exd5
11.	Rc1	Be6
12.	Qa4	c5
13.	Qa3	Rc8
14.	Bb5	

This is how Semyon Furman played against Geller in one of the Army tournaments. White causes the a-pawn to move, believing that in the future that pawn may prove vulnerable.

14.	...	a6
15.	dxc5	bxc5
16.	0-0	Ra7

Geller continued the same way in the game mentioned above. One could also play 16... Qb7 with the idea of ...Qb6. In that way Black would stop the variation that caused the trouble.

| 17. | Be2 | Nd7 |

In the game Furman-Geller, Black continued 17... a5, but after 18. Rc3 Nd7 19. Rfc1 White man-

aged to keep the advantage. Tal's 17... c4 was also worth consideration. The weakening of the d4-square is not of great importance because after 18. Qxe7 Rxe7 19. Nd4 then 19... Nc6 can follow.

18.	Nd4	Qf8
19.	Nxe6	fxe6
20.	e4!	

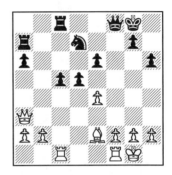

Spassky did not fully appreciate White's 20th move.

| 20. | ... | d4 |

Wouldn't 20... Nf6 or 20... c4 be better? The position takes on a character that Fischer really loves.

| 21. | f4 | Qe7 |
| 22. | e5 | |

Without paying attention to the harmless passed black d-pawn, White's Bishop is considerably stronger than his opponent's Knight. Fischer is planning to start his attack on the kingside.

| 22. | ... | Rb8 |
| 23. | Bc4 | Kh8 |

The Black position doesn't look good. On 23... Nb6 there could follow 24. Qxc5 Nxc4 25. Qxc4 and if

25... Rxb2 then 26. Qxd4 or 26. f5 Qg5 with a counterattack. 26... Rab7 loses. 26... Rxa2 27. f5! Rd7 28. f6! offers Black little hope.

| 24. | Qh3 | Nf8 |

24... Rxb2 was worth a look.

| 25. | b3 | a5 |
| 26. | f5! | |

The final part of the game, played very strongly by Fischer, can serve as a study of attacks on the King.

26.	...	exf5
27.	Rxf5	Nh7
28.	Rcf1	Qd8
29.	Qg3	Re7
30.	h4	Rbb7
31.	e6!	Rbc7
32.	Qe5	Qe8
33.	a4	

Fischer foresees even such possibilities as the move a5-a4, though in this case Spassky didn't get any relief.

33.	...	Qd8
34.	R1f2	Qe8
35.	R2f3	Qd8
36.	Bd3	

Also playable was 36. Rf7.

| 36. | ... | Qe8 |
| 37. | Qe4 | |

With the idea of 38. Rf8†!

37.	...	Nf6
38.	Rxf6	gxf6
39.	Rxf6	Kg8
40.	Bc4	Kh8
41.	Qf4	

Black resigns.

In the seventh game the World Champion had some opening chances but ended up in a losing position; in the eighth he played poorly, and lost; the ninth he drew. In the tenth, a Spanish Game, Fischer had a marvelous victory and the score became an intimidating 3½—6½ in the Challenger's favor. Back then Bent Larsen gave an interview to the correspondent of *Moskovsky Komsomoletz:*

Bent Larsen at Lone Pine

Larsen: Many people praise the sixth game. Fischer even called it the best in the match. I do not share this opinion. The only thing that I don't understand is how could Spassky have demonstrated his lack of knowledge in an opening, which his second, Grandmaster Geller, was an expert.

Correspondent: How can you characterize Spassky's game?

Larsen: So far I can not recognize the World Champion. I believe that the pre-tournament scandal orchestrated by Fischer really has taken its toll on Spassky. One of Spassky's advantages I believed, was his stronger nervous system. But Fischer did everything possible to equalize their chances.

R. Fischer-B. Spassky
Reykjavik 1972
RUY LOPEZ C95

1.	e4	e5
2.	Nf3	Nc6
3.	Bb5	a6
4.	Ba4	Nf6
5.	0-0	Be7
6.	Re1	b5
7.	Bb3	d6
8.	c3	0-0
9.	h3	Nb8

Black develops slowly but in the right direction. The Breyer is one of the popular variations of the Spanish Game that became common practice in tournaments, recommended by Furman and Borisenko.

10.	d4	Nbd7
11.	Nbd2	Bb7
12.	Bc2	Re8

The middlegame was favorable for Spassky, but later on the World Champion, obviously comfortable with his position, relaxed, and all of a sudden there was a thunderstorm on the board.

| 13. | b4 | |

Usual here is 13. Nf1 Bf8 14. Ng3 g6.

13.	...	Bf8
14.	a4	Nb6!
15.	a5	Nbd7
16.	Bb2	Qb8
17.	Rb1!	

A tricky move. White not only defends the Bishop in the forthcoming skirmish in the center, but he also hopes to use the b-file in the future to his advantage.

17.	...	c5
18.	bxc5	dxc5
19.	dxe5	Nxe5
20.	Nxe5	

20. c4! would have been more effective.

| 20. | ... | Qxe5 |
| 21. | c4 | Qf4! |

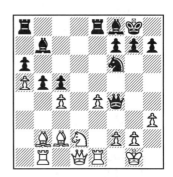

The outlook for Black is good. If 22. g3, then 22... Qh6.

22.	Bxf6	Qxf6
23.	cxb5	Red8
24.	Qc1	Qc3

This natural move is the beginning of all troubles. It would have been better to play 24... axb5. For example, 25. Rxb5 Ba6 26. Rb6 Qf4 27. Nf3 Qxc1 28. Bb3! and Black shouldn't lose.

25.	**Nf3**	**Qxa5**
26.	**Bb3!**	

A wonderful move that shows an extremely acute positional sense. Having little force at his disposal, out of nowhere, White suddenly orchestrates an attack on the King.

26.	**...**	**axb5**

On 26... Qc7, 27. b6! would have followed!

27.	**Qf4**	**Rd7**
28.	**Ne5**	**Qc7**

It seems that Black has outwitted his opponent but Fischer had calculated further ahead.

29. Rbd1!

This is core of the combination. Black has to abandon his attempts to equalize because 29... Rxd1 30. Bxf7† Kh8 31. Ng6† and it's mate in one. Also not good for Black is Rad8 30. Bxf7† Rxf7 31. Qxf7† Qxf7 32. Nxf7 Rxd1 33. Rxd1 Bxe4 34. Ng5! Bf5 35. Rd5! [Ed. Note: However, Timman follows this up with: "35... h6!! 36. Rxf5 hxg5 37. Kf1 Be7 38. Ke2 g6 39. Rd5 Kf7 40. Rd7 c4 and White doesn't have the slightest hope of winning."]

29.	**...**	**Re7**
30.	**Bxf7†**	**Rxf7**
31.	**Qxf7†**	**Qxf7**
32.	**Nxf7**	**Bxe4**

Of course, not 32... Kxf7 because of 33. Rd7† and the black Bishop on b7 perishes. A couple of passed pawns and an actively posi-

tioned black Rook does give some hope. However, further developments show that even here, Fischer stays on top.

33.	**Rxe4**	**Kxf7**
34.	**Rd7†**	**Kf6**
35.	**Rb7**	**Ra1†**
36.	**Kh2**	**Bd6†**
37.	**g3**	**b4**
38.	**Kg2**	**h5**

This move loses.

39.	**Rb6**	**Rd1**
40.	**Kf3!**	**Kf7**
41.	**Ke2**	

The sealed move.

41.	**...**	**Rd5**
42.	**f4!**	

Analysis showed that a chance to save Black was in the variation: 42. Rb7† Kf6 43. Rd7 Kf5 44. f3 g5! 45. g4† hxg4 46. hxg4† Kf6 and White has no useful moves. 44. Ke3 c4! doesn't lead to success either. White avoids the trap and finishes the game with great precision.

42.	**...**	**g6**
43.	**g4**	**hxg4**
44.	**hxg4**	**g5**

45.	f5	Be5
46.	Rb5	Kf6
47.	Rexb4	Bd4
48.	Rb6†	Ke5
49.	Kf3!	Rd8
50.	Rb8	Rd7
51.	R4b7	Rd6
52.	Rb6	Rd7
53.	Rg6	Kd5
54.	Rxg5	Be5
55.	f6	Kd4
56.	Rb1	

Black resigned.

In the eleventh game Spassky was the winner. But the outcome of the match that the whole world was breathlessly watching had already been determined.

Let's interrupt the match for a moment. The American challenger's play was remarkable, powerful, inspiring, confident and sharp. The United States was in the throes of a real chess-fever during that gripping contest. Hundreds of New Yorkers discussed Fischer's games in the bars, clubs, and parks. The magazines and newspapers allowed more space to chess and interviews than ever before. Fischer's biography and creative life were discussed in detail. Many sports, traditionally loved by Americans, were relegated to the back pages of the news.

During this match the number of tourists who came to Reykjavik increased more than usual.

Among Spassky's seconds were grandmasters Geller and Krogius. Krogius, who had a doctorate in psychology, wrote later about his impression of Fischer [Ed. Note: Covered in *Russians vs. Fischer.*]:

"It was here that I saw Fischer for the first time and carefully watched him... I noted Fischer's trim, athletic figure. In reply to questions, he said that he weighed 193 pounds and was 6 feet two inches tall. He was casually outfitted in a dark green suit. A simple necktie, short hair, a pleasant, vigorous face, and eyes that looked straight at a person... There was nothing unusual about him, except possibly one thing: he could not stand still for long and kept shifting his weight from one foot to the other...

...Before Reykjavik, his doubts were compounded by his score in previous encounters: he had lost three games to his rival and not won a single one. Fischer made the decision to play the match at the last moment, when retreat became out of the question and accusations of cowardice had begun to be voiced. Stress has to be discharged somehow, as is well

known..."

In the first six games (with the exception of the third one), the challenger was regularly late for the game by 4-5 minutes. Perhaps, Fischer consciously armed himself with a strategy used by Emanuel Lasker at the beginning of the 20th century. In the seventh game the World Champion responded to Fischer the same way. I remember how Fischer was displeased, turning his head right and left, when he suddenly found himself alone at the table. After that he stopped being late.

At least seen outwardly, Fischer's behavior seldom changed even with the changes on the chessboard; even when he or his opponent were running low on time while thinking about their next move. He didn't show any anxiety even in the most dangerous moments of the match. Most likely, Fischer learned to restrain his emotions. It's true though, that in some cases, when so much depended on his opponent's next move, and the waiting period was particularly charged with emotions, Fischer would get up and quickly go backstage. Perhaps, only this gesture could tell the fans that he considered the situation on the board to be critical.

Not only was Fischer aware of the behavior of his opponents, but he was constantly watching his opponent across the chessboard. There are several photographs showing the American grandmaster scrutinizing not so much the position on the board as his opponent while he himself was covering his own face with his hands, leaving just "the gunslot" of his eyes for watching. Spassky himself noticed the observational powers of Fischer: "He was very much aware of my lack of confidence during the game."

The widely-spread opinion that Fischer was nothing more than a narrow-minded, though brilliant chess expert, whose only preoccupation were the chess pieces on a board is hardly justifiable.

An interesting episode happened during one of the games of the match, when Fischer asked the arbiter to make a seven year old girl in the first row leave the room... because she was eating candy. That had happened before Fischer demanded that the match should be moved into another room. A little girl prevented the contender from thinking. [Ed. Note: As an eyewitness in the first game I can verify the noisiness and general bad manners of the audience, including the noise made by candy wrappers. The incident with the little girl did not happen, if it did, during Game One.]

"But I've only eaten four pieces!," the little girl started to cry.

And then it turned out that Fischer saw perfectly well what was happening not only at the board. The spontaneity of the American grandmaster shows in his comment: "It was not four, but six, you little liar!" responded the grandmaster from the chessboard. "Do you think, I haven't counted them?" [Ed. Note: This is probably apocryphal as Fischer was not known to speak from his chair.]

The 12th game ended in a draw. In the second time control an endgame arose with opposite-color Bishops.

The 13th game ended with Fischer's brilliant victory.

Spassky-Fischer
After 64. Kc3

After Spassky's 64th move, an exceptionally original situation took place. Black's Rook is locked out, but five (!) passed pawns guarantee at least equal chances.

| 64. | ... | h1=Q |
| 65. | Rxh1 | Kd5 |

Black moves towards his passed pawns in order to help them.

66.	Kb2	f4
67.	Rd1†	Ke4
68.	Rc1	Kd3
69.	Rd1†?	

Strange as it might seem, this was the losing move. A draw could have been achieved by 69. Rc3 Kd4 70. Rf3 c3† 71. Ka1 c2 72. Rxf4† Kc3 73. Bb4† Kd3 74. Rf1 Rxg7 75. Kb2 and the black pawns are no longer dangerous.

69.	...	Ke2
70.	Rc1	f3!
71.	Bc5	Rxg7
72.	Rxc4	Rd7
73.	Re4†	Kf1
74.	Bd4	f2

White resigned. On 75. Rf4 the game is decided by 75... Rxd4 76. Rxd4 Ke2. [Ed. Note: Analysis by Purdy from his match book.]

In the 14th game of the match, "the pictures" were changing as quickly as those in a kaleidoscope: first, the challenger found himself minus a pawn, then the Champion responded in kind by making a serious blunder. The result was a draw. Games Fifteen through the Twentieth were drawn. Fischer won the twenty first game, thus putting a full stop to the match. 8½—12½ was the final result of this historical match, which brought out a new, the eleventh, World Champion. *New Times* correspondent Iona Andronov wrote in the 35th issue of that journal (1972):

"This summer, at the top of current issues of American life, the War in Vietnam, and the constant increase in the cost of living, two more highly controversial issues were added to the top of the list: the election campaign, and the chess championship in Reykjavik. The chess excitement sometimes takes an upper hand over the interest in the election battle: when the televised match from Reykjavik was interrupted in order to broadcast from Washington the election of a (primary) Vice-President for the Democrats, indignant spectators grabbed their phones and demanded that the game between Fischer and Spassky be brought back to their screens. The young chess player Shelby Lyman, almost completely unknown before the event, now became a television star.

"... regretting the defeat of our Soviet World Champion Boris Spassky, we, nevertheless, sincerely congratulate Robert Fischer with his great success and we wish him new creative successes," wrote the Soviet chess player Vasily Panov shortly after the event, speaking on behalf of all the chess players of our country.

By the end of the match there was a real pilgrimage of Americans into Reykjavik. Among them one young lady showed a lot of restraint. This was Fischer's sister Joan Fischer-Targ. It was this sister who taught Fischer to play chess in 1949. When the journalist who recognized Joan, in spite of her trying to remain incognito, tried to interview her, she refused. "Ask my brother," she said. "It's he who plays chess."

She gave some information about herself: namely, that her husband was a para/physicist who worked at Stanford University, that she is not a strong chess player, though she loves chess. They have three children who have played chess since age five. "But we don't want our children," said the Champion's sister, "to become chess players."

On September 1, 1972 the official ceremony of awards for the new World Champion took place in Reykjavik. One could get a reservation to the final chess dinner only by paying 25 dollars for the ticket. Robert James Fischer was invited to come to the stage. Dr. Max Euwe declared him to be the 11th Chess World Champion, and put a laurel wreath around his neck. What followed next was long remembered by those present.

Euwe gave the new Champion the envelope with the monetary award, and simultaneously extended his hand for a handshake. Fischer did not offer his hand in return. First, he opened the envelope, took out the check, and carefully studied it. Euwe's hand hung in the air. Finally, having made sure that everything was okay, Bobby carefully put the check back into the envelope, placed the envelope in the inner pocket of his jacket, and then quickly shook hands with Euwe; after that he returned to a table covered with numerous dishes of food.

L to R: Kazic, ?, Euwe

In the *Russians vs. Fischer* we find that during the dinner celebration in his honor Bobby paid little attention to speeches and addresses, but instead, arranged some chess position on his pocket chess-set and sat trying to solve a problem there immersed in his thoughts. Krogius later wrote:

"... I had the chance to speak to him several times. We spoke Russian. Fischer told me that he was learning Russian because he felt it necessary to study the Russian chess literature in the original. He added that he did not trust translations. To be sure, Fischer's Russian was far from perfect, but we were able to understand each other, especially on chess subjects."

The prize fund established for the World Championship participants cannot be compared with the one established in our time for A. Karpov and G. Kasparov. The old ones were much smaller.

In my opinion, at that time Fischer cared less about the money. Make your own judgement. He came very close to ruining his match with Spassky by demanding to double the prize fund. Why doubling it? Apparently, Fischer believed that if the prize (125 thousand dollars, and these days we're talking of millions) would be twice as high, the prestige of the tournament, and that means chess in general, could increase twofold as well. However, several months after the match in Reykjavik, Fischer refused to sign a contract for 10 million dollars for the right to use his name in an advertising campaign. That confirms the fact that Fischer was not interested in money *per se*.

So, Boris Spassky lost his Chess King title. However, once Fischer obtained the status of royalty, the world lost him immediately. In his new capacity, Bobby Fischer didn't play one single tournament or match, though he promised after challenging for the title, to actively participate in chess life, to be an active playing champion.

Many people asked the question: "Why did Spassky lose?" The answer was very simple: Fischer played better. Summarizing the match, Vasily Panov analyzed quite convincingly the reasons for Spassky's defeat:

"In the play of the Soviet Grandmaster one could sense that he didn't participate in enough tournaments. He was out of practice, and didn't have the routine the way any chess professional would have. Some said that during his participation in tournaments that Spassky might have revealed the secrets of his preparation in the opening. This is nonsense. There were no secrets that we could see in the match between Spassky and Fischer. As for Fischer, his power lie not in his detailed knowledge of classical theory or its modernization,

nor in his innovative openings (in that he was not different from other modern grandmasters), but rather in his pragmatism; in his ability to thoughtfully and economically use all the possibilities of achieving the draw or a victory..."

This is what M. M. Botvinnik wrote about the match:

"... Fischer is being tormented by fear; he is scared. Fischer persuades himself (he himself stated this) that the Soviet chess players want to damage him... He is an outstanding chess player, but apparently, he has this irrational fear of losing. One will notice the extraordinary upsurge of Fischer's creativity when analyzing the complicated position of the 13th game of the match (with Spassky – EG), *when Fischer sacrificed a piece and created a unique endgame, yes, one cannot deprecate Bobby! I am often asked why I criticize Fischer's absence of an education. This doesn't prevent him from winning. It doesn't prevent him from winning because his opponents do not use this weakness. Spassky would open up the game prematurely, and that gave Fischer the chance to*

come out dry from the water."

What did Spassky himself say after the tournament? Right after the match the ex-champion granted an interview to the Yugoslavian grandmaster Svetozar Gligoric:

Gligoric: I believe that this match was exceptionally important. The great struggle contributed considerably to the development of chess and the world popularity of the game.

Spassky: I too believe that the main thing in these matches is their contribution to the development of chess.

Gligoric: Were you satisfied with the way you played in this match?"

Spassky: To a great extent, the answer is no. Until the 21st game I was convinced that I had some real chances to save the match. At the same time, I had this constant feeling that my nerves could not take it... that I lacked the energy.... he was in my hands like a big fish, but the fish was slippery, and it's hard to hold on to it. I let him go."

Gligoric: What do you think of Fischer's game?

Spassky: As far as the technical aspect of his technique goes, Fischer is very practical. His practicality is highly developed. I realized that he was a chess player of an extraordinary power...

Spassky at work, before a big game

Boris Spassky was leaving Reykjavik upset, and he didn't conceal it from anyone. On his return to the Soviet Union he published numerous articles sharing his impressions about the match and the new champion. Of course, he wasn't always objective, which is understandable, but his statements were not without some interest.

"I found myself in the powerful illusion that Fischer was about to frustrate the match... The fact that I agreed to his unfounded request to move the match from the exhibition hall into a closed room was a great psychological mistake... Having looked through the games, I came to the conclusion that I was in a sort of fever, as if it wasn't me playing... Now that I am somewhat removed from the event, **I must say that I am simply unable to explain some of my mistakes.** (Bold is mine –EG)

"R. Fischer achieved a convincing sporting result. The quality of his game was higher, this pertains mainly to the first stage of the match. In the second stage his play looked pale. (This statement by Spassky contradicts the opinion of most chess experts and fans. —EG)"

And then Spassky added:

"What makes Fischer chess player Number One are the following characteristics: Number one, the high technique of his game. The price of each move in the opening is very high. Number two: the high level of his energy, his huge capacity for work during the match. He knows how to struggle to the very end... Apart from that Fischer is quite attuned to the mood and physical state of his opponent. His knowledge of the openings is greater than mine. (Let's remember Vasily Panov's claim about Fischer's advantage in the opening.—EG) *However, Fischer didn't have an advantage in the opening."*

The new World Champion stayed in Reykjavik for another two weeks, willingly giving interviews. He promised to retain his title for a long time: "Maybe for 10, 20 or 30 years. Maybe for my whole life."

Bobby hadn't changed his life style in Reykjavik either: he wouldn't go to bed until 5 o'clock in the morning and then stayed in bed until 3 in the afternoon. At night he usually went to the dance halls. But, he didn't dance, smoke, or drink. He would swim in the pools filled with hot springs water.

His bodyguard, policeman S. Palsson, accompanied him everywhere. Palsson once told the journalists that while Fischer was listening to his favorite pop music, he would often sing to himself. "I must say," added Palsson, "That the World Champion has absolutely no ear for music..."

On his return to the U.S., some new events having nothing to do with chess started to unfold.

First, there was a court case. While America was hailing its champion who had triumphantly come back from the capital of Iceland, the "Fox" executives [Ed. Note: Chester Fox] were filing charges against him to get recompense for a million dollars. Sometime later it was Fischer who brought a lawsuit against his publisher that would drag on for a long time. Typical stuff in the U.S.

It would've seemed that the victory in Reykjavik would have brought Fischer what he wanted, but his behavior was completely unpredictable. He avoid participating in chess competitions. He had promised to participate "two or three times a year in international tournaments for the appropriate price," shortly before. However, when the "International Hilton" offered to organize a competition in Las Vegas for 1.4 million dollars with any chess-player of his choice, Fischer refused to participate. He was offered a television show with a price tag of 1 million. Instead, Bobby asked for 10 million!

American newspapers wrote: "Everybody laughed loudly. The International Hilton laughed the loudest."

Soon after Fischer's arrival in New York he was invited to pay a visit to... one of the city jails. Strangely enough, the new champion agreed and even conducted a simultaneous game on many boards. The media didn't inform the public as to the number of chessboards he played. Somewhat dazed, Fischer moved along the chessboards with the closely guarded prisoners behind him. There were also numerous reporters and TV people rushing to immortalize such an extraordinary event.

One incident made many people laugh. When Fischer approached one of the boards, his surprise knew no limits: one of his pieces has disappeared!

"Where is my Rook?" asked Fischer.

"What Rook?" asked the prisoner pretending to be taken by surprise.

"Here, on c2 was my Rook!" exclaimed the World Champion.

Finally, the Rook was retrieved from an inmate's pocket and returned to the board. That didn't calm down the Champion. Continuing the session, he kept muttering: "It's outrageous! How is that possible? He simply stole my Rook! I'll write to the President! He'll get an additional sentence!" The guard at the chessboard responded: "This is of course, possible. But he is already serving the maximum term: ninety nine years..."

American chess life, revived by the match in Reykjavik, was booming. A month after Fischer was pronounced World Champion a new chess club, "Chess City," opened in New York. The club organized tournaments, sold chess literature, chess sets, and refreshments. The U.S. Chess Federation has also expanded its activities. Before the Reykjavik tournament there were only 20,000 registered chess players in the country (a negligible number compared to other countries). By 1973 there were already 70,000. That goes to Fischer's credit.

After the Spassky-Fischer match chess book publisher David McKay increased its hardcover book production twofold and its softcover book by 4 times.

During the match a hypnotist and yogi, Pomark from South Africa, offered to play one game with each of the contenders on TV. His bet was $150,000. Spassky was not interested in the proposal. As for Fischer's advisers, they decided to negotiate a deal.

One of Pomarks' best tricks was hanging from a rope in a strait-jacket for five minutes and then getting out of it unharmed. On learning about this, the English master Harry Golombek warned Pomark, through the *Times* newspaper:

"You may be a magician par excellence, but when you start negotiating with Fischer, you'll get a desire to hang yourself for real."

Three weeks later Pomark informed Golombek that he was right!

Many Soviet specialists (grandmasters, journalists, political and sports commentators) evaluated differently the nature of Fischer's creativity. Some of their comments were quite objective. This is what International Grandmaster Suetin wrote in 1971:

"From his very beginning, Fischer differed from others in his pragmatic approach to the game, in the concreteness and efficacy of his ideas. It is typical for Fischer to constantly perfect the strong side of his playing. His art of the middle game is constantly enriched by new strategies. What catches the eye is not only his tendency to use lines that are at present considered old-fashioned, but even systems that were long ago forgotten or rejected. For example, in the Spanish Game, he willingly uses A. Ander-

ssen's old continuation:

"3...a6 4. Bxc6 dxc6 5. 0-0; in the Caro-Kann Defense he insists on a long forgotten variant: 2. d4 d5 3. exd5 cxd5 4. c3.

"From his very beginning in adult chess, Fischer sees mistakes in the opening with an amazing perspicacity and he "punishes" his opponents for playing them. He cleverly notices the slightest imbalance in the opening.

"Fischer is characterized by an extremely high technique; he is a master of all types of endgames.

"Definitely, his favorite positions are those constructed with a certain plan of action (independent of whether he has to be in an attacking or defensive mode). This reflects the crystal clear style of his thinking."

I wonder if Spassky knew about this and the other comments of Soviet grandmasters while he was preparing for his game with Fischer? In our country there is a Grandmaster whose specialty was Fischer. Yuri Balashov graduated from the Institute of Physical Training (a special chess department), and selected Fischer for his thesis. In Vancouver, during the Fischer-Taimanov match,

Arthur Bisguier and two acting hopefuls.

it turned out that not even Fischer had such a catalog of his own games, as Yuri Balashov had.

After the match with Taimanov, Fischer tried to "test" Yuri. Yuri gave complete and quick answers about any game that the American Champion had played as far back as ten years earlier.

"He knows by heart all of my games!" said Fischer who was surprised by Balashov's encyclopedic knowledge. Then he asked: "Can you tell me Yuri about my games against Grandmaster Bisguier?"

"I don't believe he managed to make even a draw with you," remarked Yuri modestly.

"You are right," Bobby laughed, "our score is 13-0!*"

---

* for the record: Bisguier vs. Fischer contests:

• Bisguier won in 1956.
• They drew in 1957.
• Fischer won the next 12.

Several weeks after his return from Reykjavik, the American grandmaster who had been hailed by America, literally disappeared. Before that, when the Mayor of New York, John Lindsay, offered to mark the Champion's return home by a parade of marching girls and costumed actors, the Champion refused impolitely. "I do not believe in heroes," he declared. He showed up on two of the most popular TV shows with the famous comedians Bob Hope and Johnny Carson. But that was it.

For awhile Fischer didn't appear anywhere, nor participate in any tournaments, nor grant any interviews.

"When did you see Fischer for the last time?" journalist Dimitrije Bjelica asked grandmaster L. Kavalek some time later.

"Same time as you, in the summer of 1972 in Reykjavik," was his answer.

In 1974, George Koltanowski, the head of the American XXI Olympic delegation, was asked a question as to what Fischer was doing. Mr. Koltanowski gave a more definitive answer:

"... He is an active member of his religious sect; is involved in three lawsuits and is preparing for the match with Karpov."

That was two years after 1972. And then? Fischer was hiding in Pasadena (California) in the midst of that very sect with which he would break up.

Fischer and religion? He had been contemplating about the philosophical issues of life and death for a long time. Except for chess, all his ideas about the surrounding world are vague. That may explain his attraction to religion, for the search of a "higher consciousness," the longing that has always been exploited by the "catchers of human souls."

Even before his victory in Reykjavik, Fischer was absorbed by a religious sect founded in 1934 by Herbert W. Armstrong (a former advertising executive). Publicizing his sect widely on radio and television Armstrong "recruited" more than 130,000 members into the Worldwide Church of God. The members of his sect observed a special diet, didn't smoke, and vowed never to divorce. The head of this sect was also a shrewd businessman. Through his ardent praying on radio and television, as well as his son Garner Ted Armstrong's proselytizing, he created lots of publicity for the Worldwide Church of God.

The richest members would give a tithe of 10% of their income. At one time church revenue exceeded 200 million dollars a year. The leaders owned lots of property, including three donated jets. They lived in style while the ordinary members did not.

Fischer met the oldest Armstrong as a young man. He was then 19. Shaken by his failures to become World Champion, Bobby was seeking solace within Armstrong's church. Being tired after Reykjavik, he didn't want to see anyone. And Pasadena, not far from Los Angeles, seemed an ideal place for him. A place where he could come to his senses, and calm down.

Fischer was not a full member of the sect. He was considered to be a "sympathizer." Armstrong demanded 20 percent of Fischer's earnings from the match, and when he received that, he exclaimed: "Oh, my dear boy! That is exactly what God would like to have!"

The members of the sect were instructed to treat Bobby as a very important member close to the inner circle. He was granted a luxurious three-room apartment with a gym, tennis court, a swimming pool and a personal trainer. Almost every day Fischer played tennis with his trainer, lifted weights, and when he became interested in women, he was immediately introduced to a lady. This lifestyle continued for six months. Bobby forgot all about chess. He didn't want to leave the community, even when he got a personal invitation from Kissinger!

However, soon Fischer realized that veneration of the Almighty is often of little concern for any cult. "The leaders of that sect were terrible hypocrites," Fischer's friend, Zuckerman wrote. "They advocate the reconciliation of Jews and Christians, but cannot reach peace among themselves; they are constantly at each other's throat."

Another episode in Fischer's life is worth mentioning. In November 1972 Fischer flew to San Antonio (Texas) to participate in a religious conference. The meeting of his church members coincided with an international chess tournament held in the city at the same time. Fischer couldn't help it and dropped by to look at the games. He watched the games of the Soviet grandmasters (where, by the way, young Karpov was also playing). Somebody heard his comment: "They are just chickens." After that he left San Antonio for Denver accompanied by a group of his admirers. He stayed there for some time...

After 1973 Fischer finally broke with the Worldwide Church of God.

A special correspondent for the newspaper *Izvestya,* Vitaly Kobish, wrote an article "Two years of Bobby Fischer:"

"At that moment Bobby Fischer seemed to be gradually

returning to chess. In October 1973 he came to a Manila tournament as a guest of Philippine President Marcos."

Let me interrupt Kobish's story for a moment. Before his trip to the Philippines, Fischer gave Gligoric an interview for Belgrade radio. That was the first interview of its kind after Reykjavik. Again the world heard the non-playing Champion promising, at least three times a year, to "defend his title." Bobby said that the players of the Leningrad and Brazilian interzonal tournaments were an interesting, diverse lot; however, he couldn't really say precisely which event had the better players. (This was at the time of an ardent dispute about the unequal abilities of the participants for these two events.) Fischer praised Petrosian, Karpov, and Mecking. He confirmed his desire to play for a World Championship match with the title going to the first winner of 10 games.

Before his flight, at the airport, Fischer admitted that he was still waiting for "an appropriate offer" to come through in order to start playing chess.

Fischer's appearance was in sharp contrast with the way he looked at Reykjavik: he was dressed in a conservative dark-blue suit of a fashionable cut, his light hair shortly cropped. Hiding from a drizzling rain under a big umbrella, he was smiling in response to applause; he even said in a short interview that he considered Spassky to be the strongest Challenger...

Back to Kobish's story about Fischer's stay with the Marcoses.

"Fischer made a speech. Spent a night in the Presidential Palace, spent some time on the Marcos' yacht and then left for Tokyo. A few weeks later he came back to Pasadena to his own apartment. He didn't want to see anybody except his personal trainer. His lifestyle was still strange. He slept till noon, and at night listened to the radio for hours, browsed through the New York Times, *or just laid about... For the first time in more than a year he started analyzing some games. Gradually he went back to work, and soon his apartment was flooded with chess literature. Those who saw Fischer at the time, said that a cold glint appeared in his eyes."*

Earlier Fischer made a statement to the French Press Bureau "that he was not afraid to defend the World Champion's title in 1975," that he was also prepared to play against

**Reykjavik, one of many press conferences in 1972.
From L to R: Fr. Lombardy, Dr. Krogius (?), Dr. Euwe, and Fred Cramer.**

any of the strongest Soviet chess players. With that in mind, he plunged into intensive preparation: he would read a dozen chess publications as soon as they would become available. Fischer also said that in his match with Spassky he considered the third game to be crucial, the pivotal one. Again he categorically denied rumors that he was using the "recommendations" of chess computers. (Such rumors were circulating during the match).

"My favorite openings for Black," said Fischer "are the Sicilian, King's Indian, the Nimzo-Indian and the Benoni." He mentioned that he was not trying to follow any certain style but rather was trying to find the best moves. As for his private life, he still hasn't found "the right person." He drinks occasionally, but not much, enjoys lyrical music and rock, but he doesn't dance, only watches. Now his major exercise is walking...

It was curious that during the interview Fischer easily won a ten-minute game with the future FIDE President, chess organizer and master, Florencio Campomanes, a veteran player and arbiter for the international tournament held in Milan at the time of the interview.

Autumn 1973. Robert Fischer sent a telegram to FIDE consisting of 803 words. He was protesting against the new rules according to which the Champion's title had to be defended in a match of six wins.

"That's not enough," said Bobby and suggested playing until ten wins.

Grandmaster Larry Evans explained this move by Fischer's as a search for a safety net. In his telegram the Champion expressed the opinion that with the score at 9-9 the title of the world's best chess player should remain his.

"He meant," answered Evans, "that the Challenger should win at least by an advantage of two wins, that is 10-8..."

On June 28, 1974 a UPI correspondent reported from Nice: "According to the leaders of FIDE, the organization has received a telegram from Fischer in which the World Champion informed FIDE that he forfeited the title of champion in protest against the decision of FIDE's Congress about the conditions spelled out for conducting the 1975 match. In their private conversations the official FIDE representative explained that Fischer was "only giving up his official title in the framework of FIDE," but that Fischer intended to keep the title for all other purposes and would play privately only with chess players who would leave FIDE."

Several days later, July 6 of the same year, *Times* correspondent and chess commentator Harry Golombek wrote:

"One gets the impression that the American media is quite happy with the situation created around Fischer's recent declaration. It looks as if they anticipated a burst of hysteria similar to the one that preceded the match in Reykjavik, only now on a grander scale. Some commentators express the opinion that Bobby Fischer and FIDE would come to a compromise, and that the hullabaloo accompanying the negotiations will keep up the interest of the general public to the forthcoming match... However, FIDE has already made lots of concessions to the champion and cannot continue moving in that direction without sacrificing their ideals and breaking the principle of objectivity and fairness which requires similar conditions both for the Champion and the Challenger..."

So what did we end up with? A non-playing Champion starting once again his psychological "experiments?" This was one possibility. As we know, he started preparing for the match believing that he would confront again his familiar opponent, Boris Spassky. But the world chess arena had unexpectedly changed.

In July 1974 the Western German newspaper *Unsere Zeit* reporter M. Fals wrote that in a response to

73

Fischer's request, the members of the American Olympic team in Nice were mailing to Fischer all the games played by the leader of the Soviet team Anatoly Karpov. These mailings did not stop even after Fischer had given up his official title of Champion.

Here is an excerpt from an interview given by FIDE President M. Euwe to Yugoslavian Grandmaster A. Matanovic for the newspaper *Politika:*

Matanovic: "Fischer used to criticize the World Champions because they didn't play enough. How can you explain his present passivity?"

Euwe: "Fischer changes his opinions all too often."

Matanovic: "Who has better chances with Fischer: Korchnoi or Karpov?"

Euwe: "Judging by previous results, Karpov has better chances."

Matanovic: "What would you say about the idea of organizing a tournament in two stages with the participation of Euwe, Botvinnik, Smyslov, Tal, Petrosian, Spassky and Fischer?"

Euwe: "I can only tell you who would be first in this tournament, and who would be last. Fischer would be first, Euwe, last..."

American Grandmaster W. Lombardy, who knew Fischer well, described him as a "riddle wrapped in an enigma." Lombardy characterized his behavior in Reykjavik as beyond comprehension, deprived of logic or coherence. He repeated these same characteristics of Fischer years later.

However, some people in the U.S. approved of Fischer's behavior completely and agreed with everything he had done. Sports commentator Foreman Jacobson of the *Des Moines Register* belonged to that camp. He proposed to declare Fischer no less than a non-playing chess champion for life... He wrote:

"Through his exceptional merits Bobby deserved to keep the chess crown forever, no matter whether he intends to continue playing or not... As for Karpov," Jacobson continued with condescension, "he should be proclaimed Co-Champion, and should be obliged to confirm the title once every three years."

Fischer kept refusing to play in tournaments. He didn't play for the American team in the Nice Olympiade of 1974. There were rumors that before the event he put out an ultimatum in front of the organizers demanding a separate room for himself. The French refused to cooperate. Commenting on this case, the captain of the American team, Ed Edmonson, said that if Bobby had received a separate room, he would have asked for something else....

An interesting coincidence: at the same time as the Olympics were being held in Nice, in Pasadena, where Fischer was residing, an international tournament, something seldom seen in the U.S., was taking place. Svetozar Gligoric, the eventual winner, was trying to persuade Fischer to show up, even briefly, at this tournament. Fischer kept refusing, but finally agreed. He made it to the building where the tournament was held, lingered a bit at the entrance, then, turned around and walked away.

What was it? His reluctance to see people or his fear of chess?

We will never find out. And yet, Fischer continued to prepare for the forthcoming match.

We are going to interrupt our story about Fischer's preparation for his new opponent, Anatoly Karpov. Quoting, as examples, three games from different periods, let's see how Bobby perfected his skills over the chessboard.

1962. The 17th Olympiad in Varna, Bulgaria. Fischer is only 19. His meeting with Miguel Najdorf, chess veteran, is a brilliant achievement for the young American grandmaster. They said that as Najdorf was leaving the chessboard he said, "I played like a genius. I even lost to Fischer like a genius."

R. Fischer–M. Najdorf
Varna 1962
NAJDORF SICILIAN DEFENSE B90

1.	e4	c5
2.	Nf3	d6
3.	d4	cxd4
4.	Nxd4	Nf6
5.	Nc3	a6
6.	h3	b5!?
7.	Nd5	Bb7
8.	Nxf6†	gxf6
9.	c4	bxc4
10.	Bxc4	Bxe4
11.	0-0	d5
12.	Re1	e5
13.	Qa4†!	Nd7
14.	Rxe4!	dxe4
15.	Nf5!	Bc5
16.	Ng7†!	Ke7
17.	Nf5†	Ke8
18.	Be3	Bxe3
19.	fxe3	Qb6
20.	Rd1	Ra7

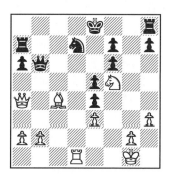

21.	Rd6!	Qd8
22.	Qb3	Qc7
23.	Bxf7†	Kd8
24.	Be6	

Black resigned. If 24... Rb7, then
25. Qd5 Qc8 26. Qa5† Ke8 27.
Rxa6 wins.

R. Fischer-O. Celle
California 1964
EVANS' GAMBIT C51

Fischer is 21. His technique had
acquired strength, accomplishment,
and power.

1.	e4	e5
2.	Nf3	Nc6
3.	Bc4	Bc5
4.	b4	Bxb4
5.	c3	Be7
6.	d4	d6?

A mistake. The correct move was
6... Na5! 7. Nxe5 Nxc4 8. Nxc4 d5!
with equal chances!)

7.	dxe5	Nxe5
8.	Nxe5	dxe5
9.	Qh5	

Much stronger than 9. Qb3, with
the possible response of 9... Be6 10.
Bxe6 fxe6 11. Qxe6 Qd3.

9.	...	g6
10.	Qxe5	Nf6
11.	Ba3	Rf8

11... Kf8 is not good because of
12... Qxf6!.

12.	0-0	Ng4
13.	Qg3	Bxa3
14.	Nxa3	Qe7
15.	Bb5†!	c6

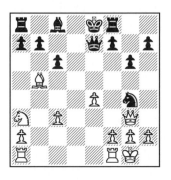

16.	Nc4	Qe6

If 16... cxb5 17. Nd6† then
White has a strong attack after 17...
Kd8 18. Rfd1 Bd7 19. Nxb7† Kc8
20. Nd6† Kd8 21. Rd4! Ne5 22.
Rad1 Kc7 23. f4 Ng4 24. h3 Nf6
25. f5 Kb6 26. Qe3 Kc7 27. Rc4†!
bxc4 28. Qc5† Bc6 29. Nb5†,
Fischer.

17.	Rad1	cxb5
18.	Qc7	Bd7
19.	Nd6†	Ke7
20.	Nf5†!	gxf5
21.	exf5	Rac8

If 21... Qxf5, then 22. Qd6† Ke8
(or 22... Kd8 23. Qxf8† Kc7 24.
Qxa8) 23. Rfe1† Be6 24. Qd7#, or
23... Qe6 24. Qxd7#.

22.	Rxd7†!	Qxd7
23.	f6†!	Nxf6
24.	Re1†!	Ne4

Effectively, the end. Black will
lose the Queen and Knight and then
resign.

R. Fischer-J. Rubinetti
Palma de Mallorca 1970
SICILIAN DEFENSE B87

Robert Fischer was 27 years old. His creativity was at its peak and he would train intensively for his match with Spassky. He easily defeated all of his opponents.

1.	e4	c5
2.	Nf3	d6
3.	d4	cxd4
4.	Nxd4	Nf6
5.	Nc3	e6
6.	Bc4	a6
7.	Bb3	b5
8.	0-0	Bb7
9.	Re1	Nbd7
10.	Bg5	h6
11.	Bh4	Nc5
12.	Bd5!!	exd5
13.	exd5†	Kd7

On 13... Be7 there would follow 14. Nf5!.

14.	b4	Na4
15.	Nxa4	bxa4
16.	c4	Kc8
17.	Qxa4	Qd7
18.	Qb3	g5
19.	Bg3	Nh5
20.	c5	dxc5
21.	bxc5	Qxd5
22.	Re8†	Kd7
23.	Qa4†	Bc6
24.	Nxc6	

Black resigned.

After 1972, Bobby "rebuked his attackers" and "attacked himself" by participating in several lawsuits. As we know, the Yugoslavian journalist Bjelica was Fischer's friend, but this friendship came to an end when Bobby filed a lawsuit against him. The dispute was precipitated by the Yugoslavian journalist using some excerpts from his book, *Grandmasters in Profile,* for publication in the youth magazine *Plavi Vesnik.* The excerpts contained stories about Fischer's life and there was something that the Grandmaster disliked. Immediately he asked for $2,000 for defamation of character damages.

L to R: B.H. Wood, Bjelica, Gligoric

But the editorial staff declared that while Fischer was simply telling his story, it was Bjelica who was the real author of the book, and that the honorarium he got was negligible, only $100. After which Fischer, through his own lawyers, sued Bjelica for... $3000!

"The game is presently postponed," wrote Bjelica at that point, "but I think I have the advantage." He was mistaken. A year before the

Spassky-Fischer match, the Zagreb Court ruled in Fischer's favor, declaring that Fischer's name was defamed. The court fined Bjelica and the magazine 10,000 dinars.

In 1972, Bobby became friendly with Brad Darrach and, in some intimate conversations, expressed to him ideas and opinions that "could not be made public." Fischer's naïveté would trick him more than once in the future. Brad Darrach, a correspondent for *Time-Life International*, styling himself as Fischer's biographer, published the book *Bobby Fischer Versus the Rest of the World*. In spite of the "oral and written assurance" to keep private conversations with Bobby a secret, he nevertheless, made them public. Fischer filed a lawsuit against him in a New York court. The case was dismissed. After 1972 the lawsuit against Darrach and "Doubleday" and "Stein and Day Publishers Inc." moved to Los Angeles. Fischer asked for 20 million dollars for defamation of his character.

According to the American press, on November 25, 1975 Judge Matthew Byrne rejected the defendants' request to cancel the case and allowed Fischer to file the lawsuit for the second time in Los Angeles.

I've already mentioned that Fischer also had filed a lawsuit against Chester Fox's production company at the very time, when af-

ter his victory in Reykjavik, the whole country was hailing him as Champion. The company was seeking a forfeit of one million dollars (a considerable sum of money compared to the award of $150,000 that Fischer had received for his victory in the match with Spassky.)

What happened? Before Reykjavik, Fischer made a deal with Fox, who had bought all the rights for filming the tournament for television directly from the room in which Fischer was to play. During the game Fischer felt that the filming was interfering with his thinking. He ordered the photographic crew to get lost.

Now was Fischer preparing for a match with Anatoly Karpov? Yes, for a certain period of time he was ready to meet Karpov at the chessboard. Though, according to *Newsweek*, it was pointed out that after Reykjavik Bobby didn't participate in a single event. In 1974 Fischer locked himself in his apartment in Southern California in order to prepare for his match with... Boris Spassky. For a long time Fischer thought that Spassky would again be his opponent.

However, another Soviet chessplayer, Grandmaster Anatoly Karpov, emerged as the Challenger.

Karpov was born in the town of Zlotoust on May 23, 1951. In 1966 he earned the title of Master of Sport, and in 1970 he became an International Grandmaster. In 1969 young Karpov became the World Junior Champion. The talented Karpov had one victory after another. An international tournament in Hastings (1971 and 1972, first and second places); victory on Board Two at the National Olympics in Moscow; first place on Board One at the XIX Students' Olympics in Graz, Austria and at the XX World Olympics in Skopje, Yugoslavia, as the first Reserve.

Having won the quarter-final candidates' match from Polugaevsky, as well as the semi-final from Spassky (at which point Bobby abandoned the idea of meeting his old opponent, and probably decided to do his best to sabotage his own participation in the match); and then winning the final match with Korchnoi in Moscow. Grandmaster Anatoly Karpov approached the owner of the world chess throne face to face:

"Neither he, nor I, remembered anything about our first meeting," reminisced Anatoly Karpov. "It happened either at the end of 1959 or at the beginning of 1960 in Chelyabinsk.

L to R: Donner, Golombek, and Karpov at Euwe's birthday 75th party in Amsterdam, 1976.

It's easy to calculate that at the time I was turning nine. I was already playing in the second category qualification and was regularly coming to Chelyabinsk to participate in the tournaments. And during one of those visits I came across a book in a book store describing the Candidates' Matches in Bled-Zagreb-Belgrade.

"I want to emphasize again: it was a remarkable book! Somehow until today I never mentioned it. I remember leafing through that book. There were photographs of eight

Candidates. Friendly carica-
tures. Robert Fischer was one
of the eight. The only remark-
able thing for me was his age.
He was 16! On that photograph
he looked angular, awkward,
his hair closely cut.

"So my first encounter with
Fischer, or rather with his cre-
ative work, passed unnoticed.
I already knew his name. The
information connected with
him was stored in my memory,
creating an extraordinary im-
age of a player.

"On the one hand, it was
clear that Fischer was unique-
ly talented... He wasn't yet the
Fischer who, several years
later, would wipe everything
and everybody off his path;
whose games were believed to
contain a special secret, a phil-
osopher's stone of chess, of
sorts... However, in our coun-
try all these facts were not re-
ally emphasized. These quali-
ties were mentioned only in
passing, they were just a pre-
text for conversation. The con-
versation itself was always re-
volving around Fischer's per-
sonality and behavior, and
around his eccentricities. To
discuss those qualities of his
became almost acceptable.
This level of conversation is of
course much easier than an at-

tempt to understand the game,
the style and the principles of
the talented chessplayer.

"His personal life is his pri-
vate matter. I would probably
not call him limited. I would
rather call him very goal ori-
ented, a man of integrity."

I must admit when I read, for the
first time, these lines of the future
World Champion, I was grateful to
Karpov. His respect for his future
opponent (and at that point Karpov
didn't know that their contest for the
chess crown would not happen),
later changed into regret about the
match that had never taken place.

Lots of people described Robert
Fischer as someone who is psychologically unstable, and has no control over his emotions. I will come
back to that later, but for now I
would like to quote one scholar: "In
our age of relativity, one can say that
the abnormal people are the norm..."

Trying to emphasize Fischer's
lack of a formal education, the following poem was composed for
Karpov by B. Guy and B. Ganin:

He matures,
Gaining wisdom hour by hour,
Fame doesn't seem to burden
him.
He caught up with Fischer in
chess rank,
He exceeded him in education,

Boris Spassky, Mikhail Tal and Lajos Portisch in the middle.

both in high school and at the university.

However, here are Krogius' words about Fischer: "I remembered Robert Fischer as a complicated man, endowed with a powerful **intellect** (bold is mine, EG).

Noting that Fischer hasn't even finished high school, some people characterized him as ignorant and primitive. These characteristics are absolutely unfounded. How can anybody call "primitive" a man who taught himself several languages, acquired knowledge and taste in literature and music, wrote some remarkable books with a logical and clear narrative, and finally reached the pinnacle in one of the richest aspects of intellectual creativity–chess?

Unfortunately, not many opinions like that were expressed in the press. I remember how the above mentioned Bjelica spread fibs about a Fischer who, allegedly, completely lacked any sense of humor. The following episodes gave him grounds for those tales:

"In one of the international tournaments with Mikhail Tal and Fischer participating (Tal was leading the tournament), Bobby thought that Mikhail said to him as he was passing by his table in a restaurant: "Bobby, cuckoo!," apparently hinting at Fischer's lagging

behind in the tournament. This was an innocent joke, but Bobby was enraged: Tal was making fun of him!

"'Why did he say "cuckoo?"' Bobby kept asking his coach. 'What right does he have to say "cuckoo" to me? I'll soon beat him. Then, I will be saying "cuckoo" to him.'

"And the teenager burst into tears..."

"Once Tal, Fischer and I were following a meandering mountain path in the car," Bjelica recalls. *"The steep rocks looked very uninviting, and, jokingly, I mentioned that if we had an accident, tomorrow all the newspapers in the world would announce that a well-known journalist with two tourists had perished.*

"Tal burst into laughter. And Bobby paused for a minute and then said: 'You're mistaken. I am more popular in the U.S. than you are...'"

So, having won from Korchnoi the decisive final candidates' match, Anatoly Karpov started to prepare for his contest with Bobby Fischer. Lots of myths were circulating in the U.S. about the young Soviet grandmaster. A great future was predicted for him.

And what about Fischer? He drowned himself in theory: developed new openings, constructed traps, and analyzed Karpov's games. Karpov still was an unknown entity, and his "psychological profile" was rather vague to Fischer. Bobby detested the unknown. Did he allow some thoughts of an imminent crown loss creep in? If he did, he never acknowledged it.

While Karpov was calm and restrained, his opponent would allow himself to say, in some rare interviews, statements like: "I'll grind him into dust..."

Bobby played a private training match with Grandmaster L. Kavalek, which was soon joined by international master B. Zuckerman.

The day of decision was approaching but Fischer couldn't find any willpower for this new trial. We can only guess at the reasons. Some secret infirmity? I wouldn't rule that out. His fear of defeat?

Fischer always found it very hard to get behind the chessboard, to start playing. The fear of failure in a world which can only appreciate success often constrained his ambitions. All these reasons might have kicked in again. Anatoly Karpov didn't resemble those grandmasters who, in the old days, Fischer used to knock down one after another. Karpov was young, unknown, and a dangerous opponent in possession of the most modern weapons of the chess struggle. The self-preservation instinct took over and made Fischer dictate unreasonable conditions for the match: the candidate must defeat the World Champion by two points. Fischer knew beforehand that that was unacceptable. Yet, he wouldn't make any concessions. He was trying to sabotage the match.

Some time before the beginning of the match, there was an announcement in the newspapers that Fischer had become involved in astrology. And, apparently, the horoscopes, foretold a Fischer defeat in his match with Karpov. An interesting detail: Anatoly Karpov was once asked before the forthcoming meeting with Fischer:

"People call you 'a second Fischer.' What's your opinion about that?"

"If that were true," Karpov responded immediately, "my match with the World Champion would be most uninteresting. What's the point of Fischer Number One playing with Fischer Number Two?"

However, Fischer never made it to the event...

Grandmaster Anatoly Karpov waited for the deadline. Midnight April 1 to April 2 was the deadline for Fischer's confirmation of his participation in the match. Karpov sent a telegram confirming his agreement to play according to the rules established by the FIDE Chess Congress.

As for Robert Fischer, he continued to keep silent...

Let's go back to 1974, the time when the FIDE Congress met in Georgetown, Malaysia, chaired by Euwe, Fischer's proposal was ultimately rejected. Fischer suggested then that there should be no limit to the number of games in World Championship matches. His second demand was to give odds. The Champion would agree to a defeat only with a score of 8-10. His opponent must gain not less than a two point advantage.

These ungrounded demands were rejected already at the FIDE Convention in Nice in 1974, which Fischer didn't attend. Instead, he sent the well-known 803 words telegram.

As for Karpov, he was ready to play Fischer. However, while Fischer was preparing for the match, he was, simultaneously, avoiding it.

"Karpov eludes Fischer both as a man and as a chessplayer, and Bobby shies away from anything unknown: the unknown annoys him and gets on his nerves," said Larry Evans, Fischer's friend. There was certainly truth in those words.

On March 18-20, 1975 an emergency meeting of FIDE was held in Bergen-an-Zee (Holland). It was called by 35 National Chess Federations. The agenda was unprecedented in the last 50 years of chess history. It was still another discussion of the demands Fischer proposed for the Nice Congress in 1974, which were rejected then. The proposal included ten won games, no limit on the number of games, "draws not counting;" and if the score is 9-9, the title of World Champion would stay with Fischer.

The Congress agreed to Fischer's first demand: "the match would be played without limit until 10 wins, draws not counting," but it rejected his second.

Manila (Philippines) was selected as the site for the next match. The deadline for both members to confirm their participation in the tournament was April 1, 1975. After the emergency meeting in Holland, Gligoric interviewed Euwe:

Gligoric: "What will Fischer's situation be if he fails to confirm his decision to defend the title of Champion by April 1?"

Euwe: "I think it would be a rather risky thing for him to do. If Fischer loses his title, it won't be easy for him to get it back..."

Gligoric: "What are the official rights that he holds in this next cycle of the contest for the world leadership in chess?"

Euwe: "In the next cycle Fischer would be allowed to participate in the candidates' matches, omitting all the preliminary stages. However, he would have to play (and win) several candidates' matches."

After the end of the emergency session in Bergen-An-Zee, the Associated Press released the information about Fischer's telephone call to FIDE.

"Okay. I will play. I will show them all," he allegedly said.

But the clock was ticking and on April 1 Bobby kept his silence.

Then Euwe, who was trying to save the match (the way he did in Reykjavik in 1972), extended Fischer's deadline for another day. That decision was announced at a special meeting on April 2.

On April 3, Soviet grandmaster Anatoly Karpov was declared the 12th World Chess champion.

Commenting on Fischer's abandonment of chess, Karpov said:" I assume that Fischer simply couldn't take the gigantic strain that chess contests at the higher level require."

Somebody mentioned once that Bobby Fischer brought to chess the style of the boxer Muhammed Ali. As we know, the latter always rejected the mere thought of a defeat, something that, nevertheless, didn't help him to retain the crown in the boxing world.

So Fischer lost the title as the best chessplayer. But what about the prestige? Time worked against Fischer. With Karpov's blaring victories as the background, Fischer's silence was perceived as a sign of weakness. Fischer then began his activities in another sphere, unconnected with FIDE. In August 1975 he arranged a friendly match with Henrique Mecking. The Brazilian had already written a book about Spassky–Fischer. "Did your book sell?," Mecking was asked. "Oh, my book was as much in demand as bikinis at the Copacabana on a hot summer day!," boasted the Brazilian grandmaster.

The mediators for this meeting, the Venezuelans (the Philippine chessplayers were the organizers) had invited Fischer and Mecking to Caracas.

Fischer came to the capital of Venezuela slightly changing his appearance (he grew a mustache and a beard, and dyed them red) so as to not be recognized by journalists and fans, the lovers of autographs. But the negotiations about the match with Mecking were suddenly interrupted. When Fischer realized that his efforts at disguise didn't help, he suddenly lost his temper and disappeared from the hotel, destination unknown.

Later, two-time U.S. champion Walter Browne challenged Fischer by suggesting he play, but Fischer didn't 'pick up the glove.'

In Japan Bobby started negotiations with Karpov proposing to play in Tokyo under the following financial arrangements: the prize would be 2 million dollars. The winner would get half of that, the loser a tenth, and the rest would cover the expenses of the participants, seconds and the referees. However, Fischer was also keeping the right to chose another place for the game if someone came up with more money... This match never took place. Nor did the one with Svetozar Gligoric which had been negotiated in 1978.

I remember how in 1966 Bobby Fischer and Leonid Stein met in Havana as friends at the XVII Olympiad.

"You're the Champion of the U.S.S.R., and I am the Champion of the U.S.A. Let's play a match!"

Stein agreed. Fidel Castro was approached by both grandmasters for help, and he was agreeable.

"I guarantee you all the conditions," said Fidel Castro. "When do you want to play?"

"Immediately after the Olympics," said Fischer.

Stein objected. The Olympics were to be finished by November 20th. The U.S.S.R. Championship would be in one month. This would coincide with a zonal tournament and could not be missed.

Fischer and Stein failed to reach

any agreement. The Soviet grandmaster was truly surprised when some time later he saw Fischer's interview with some correspondents: "I am under the impression," Fischer said, "that Soviet grandmasters keep avoiding a match with me..."

The voluntary withdrawal of the chess genius Robert James Fischer from the world arena, at the peak of his form, upset the world's chess fans. His creativity was always attractive to the Soviet chessplayers.

Later Nona Gaprindashvili wrote: "Fischer upset the public by depriving it of such an engrossing sight, as would have been his contest with Anatoly Karpov. And she then asked the question: "Why did Fischer give up his position without any struggle?"

This act of the American champion is one of his tragedies.

The rating list for January 1979 did not show the name of the American ex-champion. The new rules dictated that a chessplayer who didn't participate in contests for three years would not be listed in the ratings. Fischer's last rating coefficient, in 1975, was 2780.

After Karpov became the World Champion, the press responded to the event in a variety of ways.

"I believe that by deciding not to play with Karpov, Fischer shot himself," pronounced Robert Byrne.

Burt Hochberg, the editor of the American chess magazine *Chess Life and Review* called Fischer's refusal to play "an invaluable loss for himself..."

The Dutch Grandmaster Jan Donner wrote in the newspaper *De Folksrant*: "Fischer didn't want to acknowledge that one cannot be a chessplayer without opponents.

"One needs competitors to remain as Champion. But for that one needs at least the minimum of agreement with others."

Najdorf wrote: "One couldn't rule out Fischer's victory. His refusal means that he is absolutely illogical. Even though he is a very strong chess player, I suppose that even if his condition to play until 9-9 had been accepted, he would have found a pretext to not play."

I also learned of the opinion of American writer George Steiner.

Steiner was convinced that Fischer never did anything in vain, that every step was well-thought out and served some purpose.

"Over the last three years Fischer visited three countries," wrote Steiner in *Newsday*. He was in the Philippines, Japan and Mexico. Each of these visits brought its own results. The Filipinos offered a prize of 5 million dollars. Japan moved to convene an extra FIDE Congress. As for the Mexican tour of 1974, that was a kind of decoy maneuver."

Soon after this trip the media announced that Mexico was going to offer a 1.5 million prize, and though this statement proved to be false, it helped Fischer to get further financial concessions from the Philippines.

Two of Fischer's former seconds, Robert Byrne and Larry Evans, believed that his behavior was mostly motivated by... fear.

Larry Evans wrote in the Washington weekly *Potomac* at the end of January 1975: "Since the time when Bobby closely approached the Chess Olympus, his soul was invaded by the fear of a defeat, unknown to him before. And if in Reykjavik he was able to overcome his fear, after he had caused Spassky to lose his self-control, now he confronted a more complicated psychological problem."

Darrach said almost the same thing. He explains that Fischer's refusal to participate in any match after Reykjavik was not only because of his fear of a defeat or his reluctance to disclose the secret of his preparation for the match, but also by the fact that Fischer wasn't sure he would be able to demonstrate the game "worthy of the World Champion" if he makes a mistake in the evaluation of a position, etc.

According to Darrach, Fischer constantly was in a state of fear and suspicion. He was afraid of intrigue that, allegedly, the "Russians" were concocting against him. He was afraid of journalists, mobs of people...

The London newspaper *Daily Telegraph* announced the reasons for giving up the match with Karpov to be too illogical, too convoluted for anybody, including the World Champion himself, to be able to comprehend. The newspaper said that Fischer put forward 63 conditions for the organization of that match.

The Reuters Press Agency once calculated that during his career Fischer won 327 games, had 188 draws and 61 defeats.

There is another interesting piece of data: the number of games played by Fischer in the major official tournaments from 1958 to 1972:

1958— 37;
1959— 80 (!);
1960— 68;
1961— 41;
1962— 68;
1963— 26;
1964— 11;
1965— 32;
1966— 35;
1967— 47;
1968— 26;
1969— 1 (!);
1970— 73 (!);
1971— 21;
1972— 21.

On average, Fischer played 40 games a year.

Robert Fischer is a genius. And, as with most geniuses, he is extremely contradictory, extravagant, and not like the rest of us. Being ironic, and sometimes too harsh in his attitudes, he immediately rebuffed anything that seemed to him to be the slightest attempt to intrude into his inner world. His response to these attempts were all kinds of fibs that he told people. For example, his desire to buy a wife in Thailand "for $200" (N. Kroguis).

In one of the letters to his friend Larry Evans, Fischer wrote:

"Maybe even now you'll try to persuade your readers that one can bring that endgame to a draw, and to prove your point you will be providing all kinds of arguments, but you can't fool me on that. In the present situation, Black is finished."

These words convinced some of the journalists that if Fischer carried out his threat and left the chess scene, the world would not only lose an outstanding chessplayer but a man with an original writing style. In the preface to Fischer's book *My 60 Memorable Games,* Fischer wrote warmly and with great respect about his friend: "I would like to express my gratitude to Larry Evans, my friend and colleague, for his invaluable help in the literary treatment of the text and for providing detailed and intelligent prefaces."

This is a complete contradiction of his customary style!

Yes, he is impossible socially; interactions with him are difficult. The story of Romero during the Spassky-Fischer match, and Harry Golombek's prophecy about the outcome is sufficient to prove the point.

Here is another episode, not too flattering for Fischer.

In 1967 Prince Rainier invited two American grandmasters to participate in an international tournament in Monaco. With one condition: one of the participants must be Fischer.

Fischer came and won the tournament. But he behaved in such a way that when two years later two American chessplayers were invited to the tournament again, the condition was the opposite: send any two players, except Fischer!

At the chess Olympics in Leipzig young Bobby agreed to a draw with the Argentine Grandmaster M. Najdorf in an extravagant way: being unable to find a winning move, he became resentful and just... wiped all the pieces off the table.

In the 1962 Olympics during his game with Padevsky, Fischer wrote on a piece of paper "A Draw" on the 19th/20th move. Bobby got up from the table, ready to leave. Salo Flohr, chief referee at the Olympics, was indignant: a draw before the "conventional" thirty moves limit? He "grabbed" Fischer at the exit; this rapid exchange followed:

"Bobby, you have to make more moves."

"I know better than all your FIDE taken together when it's a draw," said Fischer.

"That maybe so, but the rules are the rules..."

"Rules? They're not for me..." declared Fischer and ran off. [Reported in *64,* issue no. 2, 1980, by Salo Flohr.]

Once a young lady collecting autographs approached Fischer. All excited, she handed over a clean sheet of paper to him. Bobby put his signature across the whole page. When the girl pointed out to Fischer that he had left no room for other autographs, he answered "The autographs of others are just nonsense!"

People joked that Fischer was avoiding women because of their inability to play chess. He only admired one woman, Grandmaster Bisguier's wife. She, according to Fischer, had an invaluable quality: "She was able to mate a solitary King with a Bishop and Knight."

Compared to these invented or half-invented stories, some accounts about Fischer sounded much more realistic.

For example, A. Kotov (1962) recalled:

"My first impression of Fischer after I met him personally, was in sharp contrast to everything I read about him in newspapers or magazines. I didn't notice any arrogance or unpleasant familiarity about him. On the contrary, he was modest, non-talkative. Later I realized, that it was very difficult to involve him in a long conversation. He preferred to be silent. And he never allowed himself any sarcastic or condescending remarks about his opponent. I particularly admired how Fischer behaved at the end of the game. In Stockholm the tournament took place in a building with no backstage room for the participants... As soon as the game was over, Fischer would collect all his pieces and the board and would go to the cloak room. Placing himself in a dark corner, he would spend hours analysing all the possible positions together with his opponent. At midnight the cloakroom attendant could hardly convince Fischer that it was

time to go home.

"Fischer also looked different from the way the gossiping journalists used to describe him. Always smartly and neatly dressed, he would appear every day in a well-ironed suit wearing a white shirt and a modest but matching tie. Fischer could be called a dandy, rather than a tasteless show-off."

L to R: ?, E. Mednis (?), Jack Collins

The world has acknowledged the chess genius of Robert Fischer. Thomas Alva Edison, Fischer's famous countryman, used to say: "Genius is one percent inspiration and ninety nine percent perspiration." This characteristic applies completely to Fischer, the chessplayer. The fact that Fischer himself didn't believe that this was the case, emphasizes his genius in chess.

Possessing a strong intellect for chess, Fischer, according to many, did not have tact, cultured social behavior, nor the ability to relate to people. As we can see, anything beyond chess was not his concern; nor was he preoccupied with other people's emotions; as for creature comforts, Fischer was not asking for much...

Did Fischer play chess after 1975? Yes, he did. Two years after he lost the title of Champion, Fischer played about twenty training games with his former teacher, master Collins. The result: 16 victories, 1 defeat, 3 draws.

One of the *Computer Chess Newsletter* journal issues for 1977 published three games played by the ex-champion against a computer, using the Greenblatt Program from the Massachusetts Institute of Technology. This computer didn't participate in the competition between computers because it was programmed to play with a human being and did not participate "on principle" with its kin. A radically new piece of hardware was installed in the computer which allowed it to sort out lines with a speed of about 1 million moves a minute.

Bobby played the computer to his full capacity, not giving in to it a bit. In all the sessions the game continued to the mate, as the computer was checking Fischer's technique.

Greenblatt Program-R. Fischer
1977
SICILIAN DEFENCE B92

1.	e4	c5
2.	Nf3	d6
3.	d4	cxd4
4.	Nxd4	Nf6
5.	Nc3	a6
6.	Be2	e5
7.	Nb3	Be7
8.	Be3	0-0
9.	Qd3	Be6
10.	0-0	Nbd7
11.	Nd5	Rc8
12.	Nxe7†	Qxe7
13.	f3	d5
14.	Nd2	Qb4!

15.	Nb3	dxe4
16.	Qd1	Nd5
17.	Ba7	b6
18.	c3	Qe7
19.	fxe4	Ne3
20.	Qd3	Nxf1
21.	Qxa6	Ne3
22.	Bxb6	Qg5
23.	g3	Ra8
24.	Ba7	h5

25.	Qb7	h4
26.	Kf2	hxg3†
27.	hxg3	f5
28.	exf5	Rxf5†
29.	Ke1	Raf8
30.	Kd2	Nc4†
31.	Kc2	Qg6
32.	Qe4	Nd6
33.	Qc6	Rf2†
34.	Kd1	Bg4
35.	Bxf2	Qd3†
36.	Kc1	Bxe2
37.	Nd2	Rxf2
38.	Qxd7	Rf1†
39.	Nxf1	Qd1#

R. Fischer-Greenblatt Program
1977
KING'S GAMBIT C33

1.	e4	e5
2.	f4	exf4
3.	Bc4	d5
4.	Bxd5	Nf6
5.	Nc3	Bb4
6.	Nf3	0-0
7.	0-0	Nxd5?!
8.	Nxd5	Bd6
9.	d4	g5

10.	Nxg5!	Qxg5
11.	e5	Bh3?
12.	Rf2	Bxe5
13.	dxe5	c6
14.	Bxf4	Qg7
15.	Nf6†	Kh8
16.	Qh5	Rd8
17.	Qxh3	Na6
18.	Rf3	Qg6
19.	Rc1	Kg7
20.	Rg3	Rh8
21.	Qh6#	

In later years there was a report in the press that Fischer started to pay special attention to computer programming and that he even reviewed some mini-chess computers in one of the American magazines. These computers later became very popular in the West.

In 1979, while Fischer was in West Berlin for 10 days, an interview with him was published in the German chess magazine *Deutsche Schachzeitung.*

Fischer stayed in West Berlin on his way back from Belgrade to the U.S. The reader knows already that non-official negotiations were being held between Bobby and Gligoric in Belgrade concerning an unofficial match.

Bobby visited several antique shops. In one he noticed a chess computer.

Fischer gave an interview to his friend Alfred Sheppelt. "Would you like to meet the world champion Anatoly Karpov?" was one of the questions.

"I am ready to play," said Fischer, "But never under FIDE conditions."

"Under what circumstances would you agree to play?"

"As a minimum, I require a million dollars. But I repeat, I will never accept FIDE's conditions."

"The German Chess Federation intends to invite you to a grandmaster tournament. Will you accept the invitation?"

"No, so far I have no intention of participating in tournaments. I will only take part in matches, depending on who would be my opponent..."

A. Sheppelt said he played lots of blitz games and that Fischer, in spite of his six year break, was hardly a weaker player. "I couldn't win one single game," concluded Sheppelt (though, it is unclear what strength of a player Sheppelt was himself).

Fischer used to tell Sheppelt that the chess computer had a promising future...

I keep a rare photograph in my archives: during the candidates' in Curaçao (1962), Bobby Fischer is visiting a sick Mikhail Tal. Secretly, away from the doctors, they are analyzing games together.

Tal is in bed. There is a magnetic chess set in front of him. A laughing Fischer makes a move. Tal is also smiling.

"He is a not an unpleasant guy, all in all," said Tal about Fischer. "He looks affable. He is tall and somewhat awkward, with a very kind and prepossessing smile."

"Fischer is a pleasant, good-mannered guy," said V. Tukmakov who met Bobby in Buenos Aires in 1970.

As Darrach noticed, after Reykjavik, Fischer became much more demanding of himself in terms of chess. For example, he refused to republish his books, claiming that his annotated games were not "worthy of a World Champion."

As I've already mentioned, after his match with Spassky, Fischer had received lots of offers which would have allowed him to easily earn millions of dollars, were he to accept them. But he had rejected each of them. Why? Because they were not connected with chess. For one hundred thousand dollars he was asked to be photographed with a bottle of beer in the background. But Fischer said:

"No, this humiliates chess!"

"How about being photographed while putting shaving cream on your face, with a headline reading:

"Use our shaving cream exclusively! World Champion Fischer uses it!" A stupendous fee was promised for a photograph.

"No," said Fischer. "That would be a lie. I only use an electric razor."

His unorthodox opinions, yet his orthodox thinking, his unexpected pronouncements, this is what made Fischer so different from most.

The whole chess world knows that Capablanca was a genius of a chess player, almost without flaws. Now here comes Fischer. Not that he objects to the general consensus, he acknowledged the power of Capablanca, but ...

"A charming child in a chess world, Capablanca already at the age of 12 became Cuba's champion. From that time on he **enjoyed an absolutely undeserved reputation (same as Petrosian) of the greatest master of the endgame for all time... Capablanca didn't know the simplest rook endings.** *(Bold is mine, EG) Capablanca was one of the greatest chess players, but not because of his mastery of the endgame. His strongest point was to begin the game, then play the middlegame with such brilliance that the result of the game was already determined..."*

Try to find a similar pronouncements by other chess players, you won't find them!

Always kind and with good will towards chessplayers, Fischer couldn't stand journalists and the reporters at whose hands he had suffered much. Nowadays only scarce pieces of information in the press allow us to find anything at all about Fischer who insists upon complete silence. Some reports on him are truthful. Others are unconfirmed.

"Is Fischer coming back?" under such headlines the Russian newspaper *Izvestya* placed an article in 1981:

"Bobby Fischer, the former World Chess Champion is planning to return to Big Chess" informed the International Herald Tribune. *The well-known 38 years-old American chess player, who had disappeared from public view, announced to the Chess Federation, that as a start, he would have liked to play with some of the masters who are not candidates for the chess throne."*

This story proved to be false.

The Russian weekly *Za Rubezhom (#10, 1982)* placed an interesting reprint from the Spanish newspaper *Pais* (Madrid), under the headline: "Will Bobby Fischer's Star Shine Again?" The article read:

"As it became known, the Chess Federation of the Canary Islands has recently established contact with ex-World Champion Bobby Fischer and asked him to play in a match with one of the Spanish grandmasters. Strictly confidential negotiations were being held with the mediators of an international company which was interested in Fischer coming back to the chess scene he had abandoned in 1975, when he refused to defend his title of champion in a match with A. Karpov.

"At this time there is no grandmaster in the U.S.A. capable of challenging the Soviet grandmaster. In order to persuade Fischer to participate in a tournament that might be held in the city of Santa Druz de Tenerif, the Federation intended to offer Fischer an honorarium of 60 million pesetas. If he agreed to participate the money would be raised through the influx of chess fans to the Canary Islands. Fischer's original reaction to the offer was favorable.

"Fischer can be extremely irritable, ill-tempered, and there are rumors that he is in

deep trouble emotionally. However, the latter statement cannot be either confirmed or denied because the grandmaster is now in a state of a prolonged self-imposed isolation. Nevertheless, all specialists without exception consider him one of the most outstanding chess players in the whole history of chess."

Time passed and no match ever happened. Just as before, Robert Fischer kept his silence. Here is another article, this time in the newspaper *Sunday Times Magazine* (London). Robert James Fischer is named in this article among the former "stars," as one of those outstanding people of arts who left society, and immerse themselves in their own inner-world:

"...The talented Bobby Fischer won the chess crown more than 10 years ago. At present he lives in cheap Pasadena (California) hotels, going out only at night. During his night outings he distributes religious pamphlets, placing them on car windshields. Experiencing some serious financial difficulties (according to some rumors), the former chess player rejects, however, many profitable contracts. He is paranoid, obsessed with the fear of being followed..."

What is of interest in this article are further thoughts about those types of people who prefer solitude.

"The recluse always excites the imagination of people. According to psychologist P. Brown, the reason for that is the fact that most people do not accept loneliness and do their best to avoid it. 'As a rule, human beings seek communication,' he said. "But no doubt there are people who avoid contact with others because they find them either aggressive or too nosey.

"...Psychologist Bennett has his own, very original theory. He believes that the stress connected with the struggle for success in society is the major reason that causes the celebrity to remove themselves from society."

A short while later, the American newspaper, the *Boston Globe* [The excerpts in this newspaper were quoted by the weekly *Argumenti y Fakti*, 1988, December 12], informed its readers about Bobby Fischer's life, his problems and his poverty:

"...The eccentric and mysterious American chess genius Bobby Fischer spends his days in an orange bus travelling between Pasadena and Los Angeles. His former friends and opponents say that Fischer kept his love for chess and is still capable of defeating any grandmaster, but now he uses his brain for memorizing anti-Semitic literature and constant preaching against the Soviets. 'He is sick,' said one of the participants in an international chess tournament. 'He is a clever man but he is in bad shape. He has no money. He is very poor."

He spoiled his relations with many of his friends because of his paranoia and his ability "to eat everything near him." They call Fischer the "human vacuum-cleaner," who sucks up all the food and neglects the needs of others.

According to his friends, he never told them where he was staying, and was always asking them to drop him off some distance away from the place he lived, so that he could walk to his home. This was connected with his fear of being killed by the "Russians."

In the spring of 1981, Fischer, walking along the highway, was stopped by the Pasadena police. When he refused to tell the police his address, he was arrested and accused of vagrancy. He himself wrote a pamphlet about it under the title: *I Was Tortured in the Pasadena Jail.* This book became a "best-seller."

"No actions of Fischer can take me by surprise," said Wilkerson. " I wouldn't be surprised if tomorrow he would return to the world of chess. If he never comes back to chess, that won't surprise me either."

From time to time we discover games played by the great chess player of the past, which we didn't know about before. These games strike us with new insights; witnessing that Fischer didn't break up completely with the art of chess, though it's been a long time since he sat at the board.

The games played by Fischer in 1968 in Greece on five boards simultaneously were published for the first time in 1988. Until then they were unknown to a wider audience of chess fans. I believe the readers will be interested in two of them.

R. Fischer-A. Anastopulous
Athens clock simul 1968
RUY LOPEZ C69

1.	e4	e5
2.	Nf3	Nc6
3.	Bb5	a6

4.	Bxc6	dxc6
5.	0-0	f6
7.	Nxd4	c5
8.	Nb3	Qxd1
9.	Rxd1	Bd7
10.	a4	0-0-0
11.	Be3	b6
12.	Nc3	Bd6
13.	a5	c4
14.	axb6	

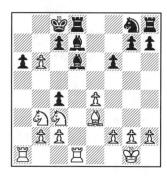

14.	...	cxb3
15.	Rxa6	Ne7
16.	Ra8†	Kb7
17.	Ra7†	Kb8
18.	Nd5	Nxd5
19.	exd5	Bc8
20.	bxc7†	Bxc7
21.	c4	Bb7
22.	Rd3	Rd7
23.	Rxb3	Bd6
24.	Ra5	Kc8
25.	Rab5	Bb8
26.	g3	Re8
27.	c5	Ba7
28.	c6	Bxc6
29.	dxc6	Rc7
30.	Rb7	

Black resigned. This is how D.

Jangos, the correspondent for the Greek newspaper *Rizospastis* commented on the game:

"A brave sacrifice undertaken by White on his 14th move proved to be doubtful. Later Fischer would say: 'I had no time to calculate to the end all the consequences of the sacrifice and that could have ended badly.'"

What was Black's mistake? Grandmaster Trifunovic believed that instead of 19.... Bc8 it would have been better to play 19... cxb6 20. Rda1 Bc8. The move suggested by the Greek Master Friganas is also worth noting. 19... c5.

Another game from this session, referred to by Jangos as "This game Fischer was supposed to lose, but as the saying goes, the strongest always have the luck."

L. Vizantiadis-R. Fischer
Athens clock simul 1968
QUEEN'S GAMBIT D50

1.	d4	Nf6
2.	c4	e6
3.	Nf3	d5
4.	Nc3	c5
5.	Bg5	cxd4
6.	Nxd4	e5
7.	Nf3	d4
8.	Nd5	Be7
9.	Bxf6	Bxf6

10.	g3	Nc6
11.	Nd2	Bg5
12.	Bg2	0-0
13.	0-0	Kh8
14.	Qc2	f5
15.	f4	Bh6
16.	Rad1	exf4
17.	gxf4	g6
18.	Nb3	Bg7
19.	e3	dxe3
20.	Nxe3	Qf6
21.	Rf2	Rb8
22.	Nd5	Qh4
23.	Qd3	Be6
24.	Qg3	Qd8
25.	Rfd2	Bg8
26.	Qf2	Re8
27.	Nc5	Qa5
28.	Nd7	Rbd8
29.	N7f6	Qxa2
30.	Nxe8	Rxe8
31.	Qc5	h6
32.	b4	Qb3
33.	b5	Na5
34.	Ne7	Bf7
35.	Rd8	Kh7
36.	Rxe8??	

An unforgiving mistake that leads to a loss.

| 36. | ... | Qxd1† |

White resigns.

While preparing for the 1972 Spassky-Fischer match, the Soviet chessplayers, needless to say, analyzed all of Fischer's games, including the ones he had lost.

Chess lovers and experts are aware of a published booklet containing all the games lost by Capablanca. This was a ridiculously thin book. In his whole life time, the great Cuban lost only... 38 games. Robert Fischer has lost over a 15 year period, 61 games (according to the book by E. Mednis *How to Beat Bobby Fischer*), but he has won many more.

Fischer's Olympiad Feats

CITY	W	D	L	%
1960 Leipzig	10	6	2	72.2
1962 Varna	8	6	3	64.7
1966 Havana	14	2	1	88.2
1970 Siegen	8	4	1	76.9
TOTALS	40	18	7	**75.4**

Fischer's defeats distributed by years:

1958 – 3
1959 – 19
1960— 8
1961— 2
1962— 11
1965— 5
1966— 4
1967— 3
1970— 3
1971— 1
1972— 2

Interesting numbers, aren't they? Let's try and analyze them, particularly since Mednis didn't.

The 15 year-old Fischer lost only

3 games in 1958. In the next year he played a lot. Naturally, that was his time of exploration, where he tried out his range. The number of his defeats, 19, indicates that. Never again would he lose so many games in one year. Already in a year the number of his defeats decreased considerably, down to 8. And in 1961 it dropped to 2. Starting from 1965, the number of the games he lost in different tournaments does not exceed 5, and before his match in Reykjavik, Fischer lost one game in 1971; two games in 1972. Isn't that evidence of a highly increased mastery of his game, the stability of the game of a remarkable American chess player?

Fischer's 61 Losses

REASON	# Lost	%
Outplayed	38	62.3
Negligence	16	26.2
Trying Too Hard	7	11.5
TOTALS	61	

Fischer's 61 Losses

REASON	# Lost	%
Grandmasters	52	85.2
Masters	9	15.0
TOTALS	61	

Fischer had the greatest number of defeats playing White in the Sicilian Defense, namely 10; the smallest number is in the Pirc Defense. Black suffered most of his defeats in the King's Indian Defense. (11).

Why are we interested in Fischer's losses? Of course, "because the defeats of a great chess master are as instructional as his victories" (R.

Byrne). The losses of a mediocre player are of little interest to anybody, they are commonplace. But when we browse through Fischer's games we can't but be surprised that even a great grandmaster erred, overlooked things, even missed the possibility of draws...

Fischer's Losses by Color

COLOR	# Lost	%
White	28	45.9
Black	33	54.1
TOTALS	61	

Fischer's strategies have few pitfalls but even those were enough for him to lose several dozen games. When he was young his recklessness would often let him down. But also, (using Mednis' expression) it could be the urgency of his desire to win. After all, in the history of chess, there has not been one single chess player who hasn't lost a game.

Now we are offering the reader samples of some of the games in which Fischer was defeated in different periods:

M. Matulovic-R. Fischer
Belgrade, 1958, training match
KING'S INDIAN DEFENSE E87

1.	c4	Nf6
2.	Nc3	g6
3.	e4	Bg7
4.	d4	d6
5.	f3	e5
6.	d5	Nh5
7.	Be3	f5
8.	Qd2	Qh4†

Loss of time, because the white Bishop is better positioned on f2 than on e3.

9.	Bf2	Qe7
10.	0-0-0	0-0
11.	Nge2	Nd7

Probably, better was 11... a5 and 12... Na6 because now this Knight blocks the movement of its own pieces.

12.	Ng3!	Nxg3
13.	hxg3	f4
14.	g4!	

A mistake would be 14. gxf4 exf4, which would give the black Bishop a perfect diagonal, and the black Knight, the perfect square e5. White's strategy is aimed at depriving these pieces of any consequential movement.

14.	...	b6
15.	Bd3	a5
16.	Bc2	Ba6
17.	b3	Rfb8

18.	Qe2	Bf6
19.	a3	Kg7
20.	b4!	axb4
21.	axb4	b5?

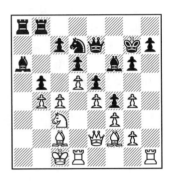

A decisive mistake! Black is constricted and unable to counterattack; a waiting move would have been better. One could move the Knight from f8 to d7 waiting to see what White would do.

22.	cxb5	Bc8
23.	Kb2	Nb6
24.	Ra1	Rxa1

Nothing better than this is available, otherwise White plays 25. Ra5.

25.	Rxa1	Bh4
26.	Bg1!	h5
27.	gxh5	gxh5
28.	Ra7	Rb7

A better attempt would have been 28... Kh6.

29.	Rxb7	Bxb7
30.	Na4!	Qd8
31.	Qf1	Kg6
32.	Bxb6!	cxb6
33.	Qg1!	

Now instead of one passed pawn

on the b-file, White will gain two.

33. ...   Qc7

Bobby makes White's task as easy as possible. Compared to the continuation in the game, Black could have saved time by playing 33... Be7.

34.	**Qxb6**	**Qxb6**
35.	**Nxb6**	**Be7**
36.	**Nc4**	**Kg5**
37.	**Na5**	**Bc8**
38.	**b6**	**Kh4**
39.	**Ba4!**	

A beautiful decoying and defensive maneuver.

39.	**...**	**Kg3**
40.	**Bd7**	**Bb7**
41.	**Bh3**	

Black resigned.

The next game was played at the XVI Olympiade in Leipzig in 1960. The 17 year old Bobby played the Ecuadorian Muñoz in a Sicilian Defense. Fischer misses the strong move 32... Bxb3! by his opponent, and the strong attack on the kingside. This loss made headlines.

R. Fischer-C. Muñoz
Leipzig 1960
SICILIAN DEFENSE B77

1.	e4	c5
2.	Nf3	d6
3.	d4	cxd4
4.	Nxd4	Nf6
5.	Nc3	g6

Defeating Fischer

PLAYER	# of Wins
E. Geller (Soviet)	5
B. Spassky (Soviet)	5
S. Gligoric (Yugoslavian)	4
T. Petrosian (Soviet)	4
M. Tal (Soviet)	4
P. Benko (Hungarian)	3
P. Keres (Soviet)	3
S. Reshevsky (American)	3
B. Ivkov (Yugoslavian)	2
V. Korchnoi (Soviet)	2
B. Larsen (Dane)	2
F. Ólafsson (Icelandic)	2
L. Pachman (Czechoslovakian)	2
W. Uhlmann (E. German)	1
M. Matulovic (Yugoslavian)	1
V. Smyslov (Soviet)	1
R. Kholmov (Soviet)	1
R. Byrne (American)	1
E. Mednis (American)	1
A. Bisguier (American)	1
D. Janosevic (Yugoslavian)	1
V. Kovacevic (Yugoslavian)	1
Others*	14
TOTALS	61
* includes many early losses	

6.	Be3	Bg7
7.	f3	0-0
8.	Qd2	Nc6
9.	Bc4	a6
10.	Bb3	Qa5
11.	0-0-0	Bd7
12.	Kb1	Rac8
13.	g4	Ne5
14.	Bh6	Nc4
15.	Bxc4	Rxc4

16.	Nb3	Qe5
17.	h4	Rfc8
18.	Bf4	Qe6
19.	h5	b5
20.	hxg6	fxg6
21.	Bh6	Bh8
22.	e5	b4
23.	exf6	bxc3
24.	Qh2	Qxf6
25.	Bg5	Qf7
26.	Qe2	cxb2
27.	Qxe7	Qxe7
28.	Bxe7	Rxc2
29.	Rxd6	Ba4
30.	Bg5	Rf2
31.	Be3	Rxf3
32.	Bd4	Bxb3
33.	axb3	Bxd4
34.	Rxd4	Rxb3
35.	Rd2	Rcb8
36.	Rd7	Ra3

White gave up.

Finally, 1966. Bobby is 23 years old.

R. Fischer-B. Larsen
Santa Monica 1966
RUY LOPEZ C82

The American grandmaster pays for his negligence.

1.	e4	e5
2.	Nf3	Nc6
3.	Bb5	a6
4.	Ba4	Nf6
5.	0-0	Nxe4
6.	d4	b5
7.	Bb3	d5
8.	dxe5	Be6
9.	c3	Bc5
10.	Nbd2	0-0
11.	Bc2	Bf5!?
12.	Nb3	Bg4
13.	Nxc5	Nxc5
14.	Re1	Re8
15.	Be3	

Instead of 15. Bf4, Fischer attacks the well-posted Knight.

| 15. | ... | Ne6 |
| 16. | Qd3 | g6? |

More solid was 16... Nf8.

17.	Bh6	Ne7
18.	Nd4	Bf5
19.	Nxf5	Nxf5
20.	Bd2!?	

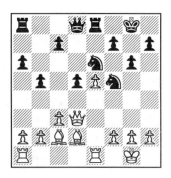

In that game Fischer was obliged, psychologically, to seek a quick victory. A normal "Fischer" move here would have been 20. Qh3!.

| 20. | ... | Qh4 |
| 21. | Qf1!? | |

White would have reached a favorable endgame on 21. Qf3! Ng5 22. Qf4!, but Bobby was always pushing to gain more.

21.	...	Nc5
22.	g3	Qc4
23.	Qg2	Nd3
24.	Bxd3	Qxd3
25.	Bg5	c6
26.	g4	Ng7
27.	Re3	Qd2
28.	b3?	

[Ed. Note: 28. Qh3! Mednis believes this is won for White until shown otherwise. Note Fischer plays it too late, on move 29.]

| 28. | ... | b4! |

If 29. cxb4?, then 29... d4, and after the Rook retreats, the Bishop on g5 perishes.

It was essential to play 29. f3, with a slightly better ending for Black.

29. Qh3??

The decisive error. Fischer was wrong about Larsen's time trouble.

| 29. | ... | bxc3 |
| 30. | Qh6 | Ne6 |

White gave up. Only now did Bobby see that his plan of 31. Bf6 d4 32. Qxh7†?? Kxh7 33. Rh3† and 34. Rh8# has a considerable drawback: 33... Qh6. In the meantime, the pawn on c3 will soon become a Queen.

Each year the world chess movement gains in popularity, its types of development changes. New "stars" appear in the arena. Sad as it is, but the match in Reykjavik be-

tween Spassky and Fischer turned out to be a treacherous and impossible trial on the life path of Robert Fischer, the American chess genius.

Many refused to believe that the American grandmaster had left chess for good. "Let's hope," said Anatoly Karpov at one of his press-conferences, "that he won't leave chess, that he would demonstrate his outstanding mastership, his talent."

Once Garry Kasparov, the 13th world chess champion, was asked:

"Imagine for a minute that Robert Fischer has appeared again in the chess arena and challenged you. How would the match between him and you have ended?"

Kasparov answered:

"A match with Fischer would be a marvelous opportunity for every chess player to test his or her abilities, including the World Champion. Only under the condition that Fischer would play the way he played in 1972..."

Truly so. The chess of Anatoly Karpov and Garry Kasparov are now on a much higher level compared to the chess of Fischer in the 70s. But Fischer's contribution to chess was enormous; he helped to make the game the way it is now. Grandmaster D. Bronstein [and G. Smolyan] believe that Fischer was the founder of the rational style in contemporary chess. He developed and implemented a new style of fighting for a win:

> *"His style contrasted sharply with that of the older generation of chess players; through its pragmatism, forcefulness, incredible directness, and a fantastic belief in his qualities as a chessplayer. This combination of traits was missing from his predecessors."*

In those earlier days chess competitions often were held in noisy, crowded quarters filled with smoke. Now the picture has radically changed for the best. Was this due to Fischer?

Fischer didn't tolerate injustices to chessplayers. He struggled for the rights of chessplayers because chess was his life, his profession, and he wanted the people in that profession to have good conditions for their work and creativity...

Having earned the title of World Champion, Robert Fischer commissioned a house in the form of a chess Rook from Austrian architect Reinhart Barnett. On the ground, divided into squares imitating the chess board, there would be a steel tower for the chess "King." Fischer's idea was that it would have no windows since the landscape would hurt his concentration, distracting his thinking over the chess board... According to the media, the project never came to fruition, but I believe that Bobby has imprisoned himself in a similar "psychological" castle while he is still alive.

Robert James Fischer is a contemporary chess legend. He left a considerable legacy in the art of chess, as well as an invaluable heritage: his own games, that, I am sure are of great interest for future generations. Fischer's tragedy, I believe, is that he sacrificed what was most precious for him: chess. Why?

Nobody knows. Chess theory has advanced in the time that has passed. To come back in order to win, that wouldn't be possible; to come back in order to lose, neither Fischer, nor his chess fans want that.

I am often asked why I decided to write about Fischer in such detail. I have only had one purpose: that future generations must have some true idea about this great chess master. We should collect every bit of information connected with a great chessplayer. I am sure, history will not forget him. He was completely devoted to his favorite art, he gave us some remarkable samples of creativity, and did a lot for all the chessplayers whose work he equated with the work of other professionals. As World Champion Kasparov shrewdly remarked:

"... The ideas, the knowledge, the contribution to theory, and the experience of five Soviet Champions [Botvinnik, Smyslov, Tal, Petrosian and Spassky, EG] *created a great quantitative resource that was about to create a qualitative shift in the manner of play, to find its new direction. I consider the next World Champion to be exactly at the forefront of this change, and, paradoxical as it may sound, the extension of Soviet chess tradition. Because he was maturing on those riches that the Soviet chess school gave the world, I believe, that modern chess started with Fischer. He understood chess on the level of the 80s... Fischer's abandonment of chess can be only commented upon by witnesses. I only regret that a match for the World Title did not take place, because it is in the contest of two leading players that the game of chess reaches its culmination."*

And when at the beginning of the 70s a decent competitor, Anatoly Karpov, emerged, it became clear that their tournaments would show how chess would develop in the future.

Karpov remained alone, because, I am convinced, the only player, equal to him, had been Fischer..."

Bobby Fischer
An Attempt at Analysis

by
Carlos Almarza-Mato

With permission from the 1999 editions of the SCCA Magazine.

The author wishes to dedicate this article to Scotland and all the members of the Scottish Correspondence Chess Association.

It has taken me over eight years to realize the importance and contribution made to chess by Bobby Fischer. It has taken me over four months to write it. This is not "the definitive article on Fischer" and the only aim I pursue is that of making the reader start thinking by him/herself, simply attempting to offer what I would like to be a new light or a different reference point to look at.

Chess conforms a vast cultural empire and sometimes it is impossible to couch in words everything one has read or every conclusion one has reached, so falling in a sort of Wittgensteinian paradox…

Chess has its own goddess, known by the name of "Caissa." May Caissa illuminate all of us in our chess initiatic paths so as we will be able to understand, discern and learn. And for her, the only words I have, were written by William Blake.

> *"What is now proved,*
> *was once only imagined."*

W. Blake

Introduction

Chess is a very complicated game.

Any player whose aim is to become a strong player, or whose goal is to devote himself to chess in a professional way, or even any player who wanted to make his way in the field of postal chess, is in fact entering the difficult realm of competitive sport. It does not matter if you want to win tournaments or become a correspondence chess GM. In both cases, the player needs systematical training. Training methods have been devised by professionals and any of us can find them in books, articles in chess magazines, etc. In my humble opinion the first requisite one needs is that of an open mind. The player has to devote his time not only to memorizing opening variations and the ideas expressed by the leading players of the moment, you need independent thought and the strength and capacity of discerning the many prejudices this world has.

One of the defects of many modern top players is that they have consciously forgotten the study of the classics. "Nobody plays like that now." This is too frequently said and far worse, I add. I have read interviews made by strong professional players who say they have never studied games played by Fischer, Spassky, Botvinnik, let alone Capablanca or Alekhine. And this explains why they will never become World Champions, or even Candidates. Take Karpov or Spassky for instance. Karpov became what he is thanks to the study of Capablanca, while Spassky's model was Alekhine. So, if the study of players who preceded them thirty or forty years in time helped them to become World Champions, how can it be said that today it is not necessary to study Fischer, Spassky or Botvinnik at the same time when you study the contemporary GMs? By accepting concepts like this, the player is simply hampering his development. An important part of the strength of a chessplayer is the knowledge of those who preceded him. In the study of the classics you will find the development of the different strategical and tactical ideas which are a part of the player's weaponry. Ideas have changed, new methods have been discovered, new approaches are used, but to know the exceptions you must know the rules first. It is very funny to see how many leading players say one thing but do a different thing. The games played by Steinitz, Alekhine, and so on can be a source of inspiration to produce even opening surprises. Perhaps some of their ideas have been forgotten, but many others can become deadly weapons if reassessed under the light of the new approaches in the field of chess strategy. With the present state of chess, and the use of computers, we must accept, the sooner the better, that the more weapons we have, the more success we can achieve. Ideas are not the patrimony of modernity. Anything which is useful, is useful, and has to be quickly integrated into our own set of concepts; it does not matter who produced it or when it was produced.

On the other hand, why do chessplayers have to study the games played by leading Grandmasters or World Champions? The answer is manifold. First, we study them because we can learn both strategy and tactics. Second, because we can learn openings and endgame technique. Third, we study a certain chessplayer because we desire to identify ourselves with that chessplayer and choose him as our model, for one reason or another. For us, he is our "master." It happens in all branches of art and there are many psychological reasons involved.

Nevertheless, in my opinion, there is one more reason for the studious chessplayer: learning the METHOD. Learning "how" and "why" our admired player produces ideas. Of course, that implies the previous knowledge of strategy, tactics, some endgame technique, and more. We want to learn his TECHNIQUE when playing chess:

• How he applies the laws or exceptions of strategy,

• How he attacks or defends,

• How he plays the transition between the opening and the middlegame, the middlegame and the endgame, the meaning of all his moves in the game, why he played this and not that.

In short, we want to clearly appreciate his PROCESS OF THINKING.

To carry out all this we have to study the player's approach to chess, the sort of positions he likes, how he reaches them, and how he tries to interfere with the opponent's plans.

So every game has to be played several times trying to understand what is behind every move. If the game is annotated, we can use the notes as a guide, although we will have to do a move-by-move job on the game. That consists of the study of chess games: the attempt to apprehend the METHOD by dissecting the games for chess is the vivid manifestation of THOUGHT.

(I would like this article, or parts of it, to be useful or at least act as a sort of eye-opener for the reader to pursue their own way. Answers only appear after questions have been made, so I'm making explicit what previously had been only implicit.)

Max Euwe: "Fischer thinks in systems, not moves. With him it is not good enough to say that a player has made a good move. You must know the system he is playing and what fits into the system."

Fischer:

"You have to force moves and take chances."

•

"Ideas, I never memorize moves."

•

"They commit mistakes."

Fischer's Chess Style

♟ Unrelenting maintenance of tension.
♟ Active play in the opening, middlegame and endgame.
♟ Concrete thinking: calculable positions.
♟ Fluid piece play.
♟ Tactical handling of defense.
♟ Concrete handling of strategy.
♟ Disciplined imagination.
♟ Highly developed ability for the calculation of variations.
♟ Alert to combinational and positionally mixed features in every position.
♟ Uses radical methods to reduce opponent's counterplay.
♟ Straightforwardness.
♟ Master in the art of switching advantages.
♟ Master in the art of playing on empty squares while always pursuing space to manuever.
♟ Does not play speculative chess.
♟ Risk and danger are calculated to the utmost, never speculating.
♟ Play "move-by-move" or "blow-by-blow."
♟ Technical perfection.
♟ Influences: Morphy, Steinitz, and Capablanca.
♟ Mastering of the twofold process of calculating variations and the formation of abstract concepts.
♟ Incredible insight for finding intermediate moves in both the calculation of variations and in combinational melées.

First Approach

Fischer's main weapon is that of his overwhelming ability to calculate variations, having a deep insight into finding intermediate moves in the most complicated of positions. The "clarity" of his play claimed by some critics, and some Soviet players, is only delusion. His play is far from clear. The aspect of simplicity hides, in fact, very dangerous elements. He is able to reduce a complicated strategy to a series of blows filled with tactical venom. He often seems to be tottering on the abyss, but in fact he is seeing everything and his moves, which are but the exponents of his strategical depth, have one aim: the destruction of the opponent at the board.

Fischer subordinates everything to the system he is playing no matter how weird or odd the moves may seem. He is always assessing concrete features, paying great attention to the tactical nature of moves.

Fischer's opponents are confronted by a player who is always ready to embrace danger, using all opportunities, fighting till the last chance, always turning the board into a minefield. It is not enough to have a good plan. It is necessary to find the best move time after time, being aware of all the possible variations and subvariations, always calculating, always assessing the position from a concrete point of view.

In his games, there is no room for waiting moves, there is no way for seeing what the opponent's plans are. Fischer imposes his own tempo by posing new threats with each move. He has mastered the difficult art of linking attack after attack, being able to switch from one target to another by means of tactical and combinational threats. The rival has to either accept it or fall into strategically lost positions, so allowing Fischer to impose his superiority this time by positional means.

Fischer's Opening Systems

The openings a chessplayer uses are the first clue to understanding his approach to chess, since the opening and the variation or subvariation he chooses lead to the sort of positions he likes best. Of course, his rival will also try to impose his own mark on the game and so we have the subtle fight which characterizes the struggle for the predominance in the opening.

As Black, his preferences are clear:

Against **1. e4,** the Sicilian Najdorf (He has played Alekhine's 1. e4 ♘f6 in a few games and even 1. e4 e5, but only in three or four games throughout his chess career.)

Against **1. d4 / 1. c4,** he has

played mainly the King's Indian or other similar systems characterized by the f-Bishop's fianchetto. In the early sixties, he played systems involving ... ♘f6 / ...e6 (the Nimzo-Indian, Tarrasch, Ragozin) but this was a transition period. Apart from the King's Indian, the Grünfeld Defense was also one of his favourite openings and prior to the Rejkjavik match he had used it in very important encounters.

Fischer's aims as Black are clear: quick equalization, fluid piece play, counterattack and the provocation of tactical clashes as soon as possible.

Being primarily a positional player, Fischer was able to infuse tactical poison into well-known, time-honored positional systems. This versatility allowed him to be ready for protracted positional struggles or for quick tactical skirmishes, thus becoming a formidable opponent.

In my opinion, the "Russians" totally failed to appreciate all of this and labored under the belief that Fischer's style was "crystal clear," "easy to predict," "easy to meet," and so on. They believed that an individual, fighting alone, would not be able to offer any resistance against the enormous Soviet chess machinery. This delusional concept was helped by the fact that prior to 1972 some Soviet players had posed many problems to Fischer (for instance Keres, Tal, Geller and Spass-

ky too). Perhaps they forgot that a loner like Fischer, who had chess as his vital obsession and the only way to affirm himself before the world, had been learning from his defeats at Soviet hands. His self-criticism, as well as his psychological insight concerning the Soviet players, his main enemies, were giving him a clear picture of what loomed ahead, while the Soviets were resting on their laurels, forgetting that past feats do not earn present points in chess matches, and that chess is a game in which two players have to meet, with their virtues, yes, but also being liable to show all their defects. Spassky's sin, and the Soviet sin concerning 1972 has two names: "over-confidence" and "under-estimation." Against a sniper like Fischer, all that proved fatal.

As White:

Here the matter is even clearer: with the exception of his early beginnings, Fischer mainly played 1. e4. He simply spoke of this move as "best by test," never engaging in other philosophical discussions. In his early years he played the King's Indian Attack and he had also played 1. b3 in some offhand games, even though one of these games was against Tukmakov in an important tournament.

As he can be considered a classical chessplayer, it is normal that his main weapon is the Ruy Lopez. From time to time he also used the King's Gambit and the Italian Opening, choosing in these two cases, variations not normally employed but that Fischer had studied in depth due to his love for players like Steinitz.

One of the recurrent themes in Fischer's games as White is that of the center without pawns. In many of his games, variations in which the central pawns are exchanged are common. It is very instructive to study how Fischer plays these positions, in which the fight revolves around piece play only.

For instance, let's take the Breyer Variation of the Ruy Lopez. Fischer consistently used the Simagin system, which implies the exchange of pawns in the center and opening lines. Later, Karpov patronized the variation with the move d5, closing the center and giving preference to flank manuevers which involve a lot of "fending" strategies. Of course, Fischer knew all this too, but he simply preferred more direct methods where he could use his extreme ability to provoke fluid piece play to conjure threats apparently out of thin air, but in fact were based upon a well established strategical basis.

The opening is connected with the middlegame and all World Champions have managed to master the transition between the two. In this respect, Fischer likes producing multi-potential positions where accurate calculation is required as the only way to understand and resolve the different positions. Thus, the opponent is confronted with the problem of choosing among a wealth of possible variations, all leading to end positions difficult to evaluate, and the paths to those end positions are also full of intermediate moves. His aura of invincibility was so overwhelming that an American GM declared that it does not matter which type of position you may have, because against Fischer you "know" you are going to lose...

Fischer's style shows a two-fold feature: on the one hand a deep purity based upon the application of all the time-honored chess principles, and on the other hand, the display of tactical blows in which every move both belongs to the system and also conforms the very system he is developing.

His primary approach to positions is scientific: he knows the openings and the sort of strategical plans involved. Then he looks for the best plan and the most destructive moves to carry it out, trying to prevent any tactical struggle. When he has to resort to defense, his stubbornness is admirable: he will use all sorts of tactical resources to complicate the game compelling his rival to choose and take risks because here lies the possibility of committing mistakes or inaccuracies. The games where Fischer had to show his defensive skills are worth a deep study. Both in attack and defense, he is ready to embrace danger to the utmost if he sees that he can calculate the risk or if he feels that the position may become so wild that he will be able to impose his refined calculation technique, seeing farther than his rival or what is more important, perceiving all the nuances which compose a forest of intermediate moves.

Due to Fischer's approach to chess, which clearly manifests itself in his opening repertoire, he tended to reach what Kotov has defined as "resolvable positions." Nevertheless, I do not totally agree with Kotov's classification, and so in my opinion resolvable positions are threefold:

1. Positions resolvable by logical plans and precedents.
2. Positions resolvable by calculation.
3. Positions resolvable by the method of playing move-by-move or blow-by-blow.

(It must be understood that it is the player himself who, knowing his style and approach, decides the sort of positions he wants to reach. Then he will choose those openings which lead to the types of positions he prefers. In the process there will be a fight between him and his opponent, who will also try to steer the game into the sort of path of his liking.)

Fischer has nearly always avoided speculative positions because the thing he has most feared is that of taking risks which cannot be TOTALLY controlled through straightforward calculation. And this is another key point to understanding his style. Strategically speaking, he is a classical player, influenced by strategists like Steinitz, Tarrasch, and Capablanca. Tactically speaking, he possesses the directness of Morphy but with a killer instinct developed to the utmost.

In analyzing Fischer's games and combinations one can see how every move has an aim. Again, this does not mean that his style is "clear" and "easy to predict" as his Soviet counterparts believed, and thus were caught on the hop one after another (Taimanov, Petrosian and Spassky). Fischer's style, like the image on a mirror, is absolutely delusive, and its clarity is only apparent once you have seen the moves. If you do not believe so, take one of his games, cover his moves and try to guess them one by one.

For Fischer there is no place for double-edged, wild positions where everything depends upon luck or speculation. Fischer does not play against an opponent like Lasker or Tal might. He plays against perfection and this makes him totally averse to speculation. He wants to play a perfect game of chess, against perfect replies from his opponent. Perhaps, like Alekhine, he also suffered a lot because "it takes two to play a perfect game of chess and produce a masterpiece." It is not enough to win the game. It is necessary to produce a completely flawless game.

Fischer mastered both the rules and the exceptions, extracting some of his ideas from the strange games of Steinitz. Sometimes he showed that some exceptions were, in fact, better than the accepted rules. He accepted that causes produce effects, but that, and here lies the paradox, some effects also produce causes.

Important Explanation

In the game(s) which follow it will be normal to find the concept of "advantage." To understand a game of chess it is very important to realize how top players are able to obtain (an) advantage. In some cases it will mean, simply, to have the initiative, that is, to be the first in creating threats thereby making the opponent think only about defensive moves or plans.

"Advantage" can be obtained through different means, for instance:

♙ Mistakes committed by the opponent which allow one to obtain a strategically pre-dominant position or tactical threats.

♙ Initiative: when the opponent commits a mistake, accepts a defensive or passive role, fails to create counterplay, etc., and allows us to carry out our plans without any possibility to react with counterthreats.

♙ Positional pressure: formation of deep strategical threats which the opponent does not appreciate, fails to assess properly, or is not able to stop due to having structural weaknesses.

♙ In the tug-of-war of a game of chess, one of the players may accept certain weaknesses in exchange for what he assesses as "compensation." Nevertheless, the opponent may manage to keep the game under control avoiding the creation of weaknesses in his own position, and after a liquidation of pieces succeeds in cashing in on the rival's weak spots (one of Fischer's main weapons and one very often neglected when annotating his games, which are more than dazzling tactical fireworks).

Advantages are switched during the development of the game (positional transformations, the initiative, etc.) and this implies a high degree of technique and a high degree of talent and imagination.

In the following pages games are analyzed. But chess is inexhaustible and the reader may find many other details through the application of their own knowledge and experience. This is what all this is about. There are no absolute truths here, only hints. Instead of "teaching," it is better to show how to learn and investigate by oneself.

Hans Berliner—R. Fischer
Western Open Championship 1963
D41

This game was regarded by Fischer as one of the games which most accurately showed his chess style (unable as he was to clearly define it). The main features are:

♙ Active play to reach a multi-potential position.

♙ Avoidance of tactically unclear melées.

♙ Timely counterattack transforming a static initiative (superior piece placement) into an advantage.

♙ Creation of continual threats.

♙ Liquidation into a superior endgame: creation of threats to a majority on the queenside (another example of the switching of advantages). In this respect, Botvinnik was a real master too in the art of smoothly liquidating middlegame positions into superior endgames, perhaps due to the influence of Capablanca's games.

1. d4 ♘f6 2. c4 e6 3. ♘c3 d5 4. cxd5 ♘xd5 5. e4 ♘xc3 6. bxc3 c5.

Immediately after White has created a strong pawn center Black proceeds to attack it. The ensuing position has a mobile pawn structure.

7. ♘f3 cxd4 8. cxd4 ♗b4† 9. ♗d2 ♗xd2† 10. ♕xd2 0-0 11. ♗d3 b6 12. 0-0 ♗b7.

Exerting pressure on the center. **13. ♖fd1 ♘c6 14. ♕b2.**

Another plan would be 14. d5 exd5 15. exd5 since 15... ♕xd5?? would lose to 16. ♗xh7. Berliner prefers to maintain the tension.

14... ♕f6.

Never allowing his pieces to interfere with each other. The text attacks the pawns, pins the d-pawn, makes room for the Rooks, covers the kingside and places the Queen pointing at White's King.

15. ♖ac1 ♖fd8 16. ♗b5 ♖ac8.

17. ♘e5?!

It would have been better to maintain the tension. White wants to fix the central position in search of active play and entry points for his heavy pieces. Fischer has seen farther.

17... ♘xe5 18. dxe5 ♛f4.

Positional theme: the Queen in an advanced position.

19. ♖xc8 ♖xc8 20. ♛d4 g5!!.

Typical of Fischer. Apart from the fact that 20... ♛xe4 loses due to a backrank mate, the concept is very deep indeed, starting a sort of pre-emptive attack.

21. f3.

21. ♛d7 ♖c2.

21... g4!!.

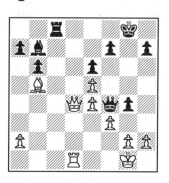

White's plan, starting with ♘e5, has failed. Fischer manages to create counterthreats with a minimum of forces. 21... ♖c5 gives nothing in view of variations like 22. ♗e8 ♖c1 23. ♗xf7 ♔xf7 24. ♛d7†.

22. ♗e2.

22. ♛d7 gxf3! 23. ♛xb7 ♖c2! (23... ♛e3 24. ♔h1 fxg2† 25. ♔xg2 ♖c2† leads to mate).

22... gxf3.

Is this move good or bad? There is no agreement. Analysts Smyslov, Tukmakov, Yudasin and Tal say nothing. Others say this is "?" and give 22... ♖c2 23. g3 ♛h6 24. ♛d3 ♖xa2 25. fxg4 ♔g7 26. ♛f3 ♛g6 27. ♗d3 ♖a4 when the black pieces display enormous activity.

23. gxf3.

Another move without agreement. While 23. ♗xf3!? was suggested, others believe that 23. ♗xf3? ♔g7 24. ♛d7 ♛e3† 25. ♔h1 ♖c1 is good for Black.

23... ♔h8.

23... ♖c2 is bad if 24. ♔h1 ♖xe2 because of 25. ♖g1†.

24. ♔h1 ♗a6!.

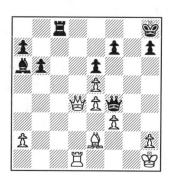

White's Bishop defends his pawns. Without it the structural weaknesses are emphasized. If 25. ♗xa6?? ♕xf3 wins. Fischer manages, through the tactical creation of threats which must be clearly anticipated and worked out by his opponents, to obtain a superior endgame. It is this process of shifting from position to position using tactical means (creation of threats), which is the key point to the understanding of Fischer's chess style.

Here, once his rival committed himself to a certain plan (17. ♘e5), Fischer started to create threats in an apparently fixed (static) position (with g5-g4). This is dynamic strategy at its best. The rest is to eliminate the defensive pieces so as to impose his superiority, a device much to Capablanca's liking.

25. ♕f2 ♗xe2 26. ♕xe2 ♕xe5–+ 27. ♖g1 f5 28. ♕d3.

28. ♕g2 fxe4 29. fxe4 b5; 28. ♖e1 f4 29. ♖g1 ♖g8 30. ♖xg8 ♔xg8.

28... fxe4 29. fxe4.

The threat is always ...♖c2.

29... ♖f8.

Fischer is trying to down his rival with piece play. But in cases like this, it is necessary for the opening of a second front. Here this second source of threats is the queenside majority.

30. ♕c2 ♕f6 31. ♖g2 ♕d4.

31... b5.

32. h3 ♕a1† 33. ♖g1 ♕e5 34. ♕g2 b5!.

The second front.

35. ♕c2 b4 36. ♕g2 a5 37. ♕c2 ♕f6.

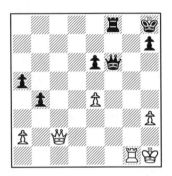

The plan now will be to force the exchange of Queens to impose his pawns.

38. ♕c4.

38. ♕g2 a4.

38... ♕f3† 39. ♔h2 ♖d8 40. ♕c2 ♕c3 41. ♕xc3†.

41. ♖g2 ♕xc2 42. ♖xc2 a4.

41... bxc3 42. ♖c1 ♖d3! 43. ♖b1 ♔g7! 44. ♖b5.

44. ♖b7† ♔f6 45. ♖xh7 ♔e5–+.

44... a4 45. ♖c5 a3 46. ♔g2 ♖e3! 47. ♖c4 ♔f6 48. h4 ♔e5 49. ♔f2 ♖h3.

Threatening 50... c2 due to the threat ...♖h2 if 51. ♖xc2.

50. ♔g2 ♖d3 51. h5 ♔f4 52. h6 ♔e3 53. ♖c7 ♔d2 54. ♖xh7 c2 55. ♖c7 c1=♕ 0-1.

An impressive game.

Bobby Fischer
An Attempt at Analysis
Part 2

The Prevention Of The Opponent's Counterplay

One of the most important parts in the armory of a top chessplayer is that of the prevention of the opponent's counterplay. It implies the realization that in chess your opponent's plans and ideas are of the same importance as one's own and that the discovering of his occult plans is as relevant as finding the best moves and plans for one's own army. (Some players, Petrosian, Karpov, Nimzovich, have or have had this as their main feature in their approach to chess.) This part of the playing method implies the existence and putting into action of what has been termed as "preventive thinking."

The difference between Fischer and other defensive players is that for Bobby this is a part in the whole of his approach to chess, and only a part, not a goal to achieve. He starts the game, realizes the strategical aim of the opening and the ensuing positions, and only in certain cases with no clear attacks or combinative operations does he proceed to apply preventive thinking, and even in this case with the intention of provoking the conditions for a direct attack, always tactically fending, always provoking his rival into taking decisions, always trying to set the tempo of the game. And he does not seek the application of this method of play by principle: he prefers open positions or positions where he can impose his superior tactical ability, and in these the most important factor is not that of "preventing threats," but the creation of them to drive the opponent onto the defensive without allowing him to arrive at too levelled or too cramped positions.

This is why it is so difficult to annotate his games. Very few of his games are deeply annotated: most of these things are neglected, are unknown or pass unnoticed by most of the annotators. Even Bobby himself has not been too explicit when annotating his own games for one reason or another. The studious player has to do it even today.

Other Processes

In chess, we can admit the existence of a two-fold process:
1. The calculation of variations.
2. The formation and handling of abstract concepts.

Everything starts with the opening. Each opening has a strategical or positional background. The different variations and subvariations lead to different positions (equal configurations of pawns and pieces). As soon as the pieces come into play, they start to create threats or fulfill missions. When the theoretical line ends or the player has to decide on his own, he has a position before him, with the pieces placed on the different squares. In some cases, he has to defend against threats or he is able to start thinking about posing threats by himself. But in other cases the calculation of variations gives nothing: it is necessary to formulate abstract concepts for which strategy can be the only red thread. And all this is not always as straightforward as Kotov, for instance, has described in his books on the middlegame in chess. The player is playing under tournament conditions with a time limit.

In Fischer, we have one of the superb masters at integrating both processes and so conjuring up a masterpiece of apparent and delusional clarity. Once again, we have to devote time and patience to understand Fischer's train of thought.

In my opinion, it took the Soviets time to understand this, and even around 1972, some representatives of Soviet chess were working under the delusion: that of his "clarity of ideas." Matches against Taimanov, Petrosian and Spassky were the signal that it was not only water that fell when it was raining: for the three,

the rain was one of stones. The same was valid for Larsen.

Fischer's fame concerning his ability at calculating variations has somehow left in the shadow another of his weapons (often unnoticed or neglected by most of his annotators): when there was no clear, straightforward plan, Fischer was able to devise complicated, elaborate, even abstruse strategical plans, by using his most powerful weapon: that of seeing in advance the nature of the ensuing positions. We must bear in mind that most of the opinions expressed during Fischer's active years came from the Soviet Union and were full of prejudices and vested interests. A simple man with limited material means (but unlimited intelligence and willpower) was able to challenge a whole super power, shouting "Check!" to the kings of chess (the Soviets). In 1972, it was "Checkmate!"

The following games illustrate Bobby Fischer's playing style.

R. Fischer—Pal Benko
U.S. Championship 1965
C95

1. e4 e5 2. ♘f3 ♘c6 3. ♗b5 a6 4. ♗a4 ♘f6 5. 0-0 ♗e7 6. ♖e1 b5 7. ♗b3 d6 8. c3 0-0 9. h3 ♘b8

10. d4 ♞bd7 11. ♞h4.

One of Fischer's preferred strategical weapons. He has always liked clear, fixed structures with fluid play and which could lead to the opening up of the position.

11... ♞b6 12. ♞d2 c5 13. dxc5 dxc5.

Opening the d-file. Apparently in contradiction to accepted strategical principles, Fischer is going to start a flank attack with an open center. But concrete factors are of paramount importance: the battle to coordinate one's pieces to create threats forcing the opponent to uncoordinate his when answering the threats. Black's pieces lack clear targets while Fischer is working with dynamic factors: the initiative.

14. ♝f5.

Thematic. The Knight hits e7 and g7. Fischer's plan is an all-out attack on the kingside.

14... ♝xf5.

14... c4 15. ♝c2 ♝xf5 16. exf5 ♛c7 17. ♛f3 ♜ad8 18. ♞e4 ♞xe4 19. ♝xe4=.

15. exf5.

15... ♛c7?!.

15... Nbd7.

16. g4!.

Fischer's own hallmark.

16... h6.

Black cannot react in the center. His pieces had to answer to concrete threats of immediate dangers. He has no pawn thrusts and White has a clear plan.

17. h4 c4 18. ♝c2 ♞h7 19. ♞f3!.

By attacking e5 White forces ...f6 thereby depriving the N/h7 from the f6 square. Subtle.

19... f6 20. ♞d2! ♜ad8 21. ♛f3 h5?.

A mistake. Except when concrete factors appear, it is not advisable to touch the pawns on the side which is under attack—an old unwritten rule. Perhaps 21... ♜d7. Passive defense is called for although against Fischer...

22. gxh5 ♞d5.

To bring the Knight over to the kingside.

23. ♞e4 ♞f4 24. ♝xf4 exf4 25. ♚h1.

Threatening ♜g1.

25... ♚h8 26. ♜g1 ♜f7 27. ♜g6 ♝d6?!.

27... ♝f8!?.

28. ♜ag1.

The culmination of the plan initiated with 14. ♞f5 and the subsequent pawn attack.

28... ♝f8 29. h6 ♛e5 30. ♛g4

♖dd7 31. f3 ♗c5.

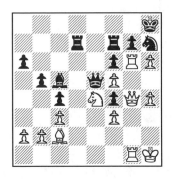

Black is in *zugzwang*.

32. ♘xc5 ♕xc5 33. ♖xg7 ♖xg7 34. hxg7† ♔g8 35. ♕g6.
Threatening 36. ♕xh7 ♔xh7 37. g8=♕.

35... ♖d8 36. ♗e4 ♕c8 37. ♕e8† 1-0.

Let us look again at move 15 in the diagrammed position, if Black plays 15... ♘bd7 the plan of g4-♘f3-h4 would not work due to the fact that h4 is under attack. But White is not compelled to start the pawn avalanche at once: 16. g4 h6 17. h4 c4 18. ♗c2 ♘h7 19. ♘f3 ♗xh4 20. ♘xh4 ♕xh4 21. ♕xd7 ♕xg4† and it is a draw. Instead he can opt for a different approach: ♗c2 with the idea of ♘f3 increasing the pressure and keeping the plan g4-g5-h4 up his sleeve.

I have chosen this hard-fought game to exemplify Fischer's skill in the field of defense. The game fea-

tures different alternatives which show how close to the wind top chessplayers sail. Very often the securing of an advantage or the loss of it depends upon a single move and more when the players are playing in dynamic fashion.

Robert Byrne—Fischer
U.S. Championship 1959-60
D41

1. d4 ♘f6 2. c4 e6 3. ♘c3 d5 4. cxd5 ♘xd5 5. ♘f3 c5 6. e3 ♘c6 7. ♗c4.
Another try would be 7. ♗d3 cxd4 8. exd4 ♗e7 9. 0-0 0-0 10. a3 etc.

7... ♘xc3 8. bxc3 ♗e7 9. 0-0 0-0 10. ♕e2.
Books say ± here but Black has a flexible position and as Tarrasch would say, "It is not only necessary to be a good chessplayer, you must play well too." With the assessments provided by books and experts it happens much the same: given any position you have to find the best moves/plans so as not to lose the advantage.

10... b6 11. ♖d1 ♕c7 12. e4 ♗b7.

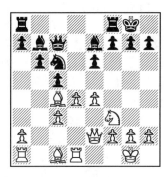

13. &e3.

These positions demand deep strategical knowledge. Byrne prefers to keep the tension in the centre without committing himself. A different approach to the position would be 13. d5!? exd5 14. &xd5 &f6 15. e5!? &ae8 16. &f4. The process of decision-making in positional games implies that the player has to clearly assess the end-positions resulting from the different variations. After all, the players have to work everything out in their minds.

13... &ac8 14. &d3 cxd4 15. cxd4.

White has a mobile pawn center and he will have to choose among three possible plans: e5, d5, or not touching the pawns. All strategy books and time-honored games by Botvinnik, Spassky, Keres, and the like show how to handle (or not!) these positions.

15... &a3?!.

Perhaps &fd8 instead. In these positions, Black has to make do with the limited space within his first three ranks.

16. e5!.

Byrne decides to open lines against Black's King, fixing the center and forgetting about dynamic tries based upon the d5 advance.

16... &b4 17. &g5.

17. &xh7?? &xh7 18. &g5† &g8 19. &h5 &c2-+.

17... h6 18. &h7† &h8 19. &h5 &d5 20. &d3 &e7.

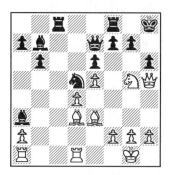

21. &h7.

21. &d2 &b4 22. &h7 &xd2 23. &xf8 &f4 24. &g4 &xd3 25. &xd2 &b4 26. &xe6 fxe6∓.

21... &xe3.

22. &xh6 must be prevented.

22. fxe3 &fd8 23. &f1 &d7 24. h4!.

To prevent ...&xg5 when trying to liberate the Knight.

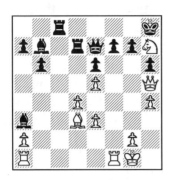

24... ♖c3!

Fischer combines passive defense with the activity of his free-from-task pieces.

25. ♘g5 ♖xd3 26. ♖xf7?!

26. ♘xf7† ♔g8 *[Ed.: Fischer "might've" played 26... ♔h7 and tried to win with a preponderance of material.]* 27. ♕g6 ♖d2 28. ♘xh6 ♔h8=.

26... ♖d2! 27. e4.

Threatening ♕g6 winning. If 27. ♖xe7 ♖xg2† 28. ♔f1 ♖xe7 29. ♘h3 *[Ed.: Perhaps 29. d5.]* ♖h2 30. ♘f2 ♔g8 and Black emerges.

27... ♕xf7 28. ♘xf7† ♖xf7 29. ♕xf7 ♗xe4.

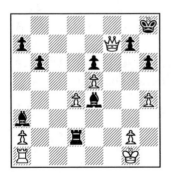

30. ♖e1.

30. ♕xe6 ♗b2 31. ♖e1 ♗xd4† 32. ♔h2 ♗xg2 33. ♖d1! ♗xe5† 34. ♕xe5 ♖xd1 35. ♔xg2+—.

30... ♖xg2† 31. ♔f1 ♗d5 32. ♖e2 ♖g4?

Analysis showed that 32... ♖xe2 was best. In these sorts of positions, the player of the black pieces may feel averse to exchanges. 32... ♖xe2 33. ♔xe2 ♗xa2 34. ♕xa7 ♗c4† 35. ♔e3 ♗f8 36. ♕xb6 ♔g8 37. ♕a7 ♗b3 38. ♔d3 ♗d5 39. ♔c3 ♗f3 40. ♔b3 ♗d1† 41. ♔c4 ♗e2†=. [Ed.: Winning is 36. ♕f7 ♗b4 37. ♕e8†! ♔h7 38. ♕a4.]

33. ♖c2 ♔h7 34. h5 ♖g5 35. ♗e2?

It is White's turn to err. 35. ♕xa7 would have been much better. Probably both players were tired and short of time after so tense a struggle.

35... ♖g2† 36. ♔d3 ♖g3† 37. ♔e2 ♖g2† 38. ♔e3 ♖g3† 39. ♔f2 ♖g5 40. ♔e2 ♖g2 ½.

R. Fischer—Fridrik Ólafsson
Mar del Plata, 1960
B52

⚠ Positional tension in a semi-open/open position with piece pressure.

⚠ Domination on the queenside.

⚠ Creation of weaknesses.

⚠ Attack on the dark squares.

♙ Massive exchange of pieces to stress Black's weaknesses and to increase White's attack over the dark squares.

♙ Switching the offensive from the queenside to the center through the domination of the dark squares.

**1. e4 c5 2. ♘f3 d6 3. ♗b5†
♗d7 4. ♗xd7†.**

Some authors believe that the early exchange of Bishops prevents the apparition of too strong a tension in the position. This is why it is admirable to see how Fischer manages to create tension in the position.

4... ♕xd7 5. 0-0 ♘c6 6. ♕e2.

Or 6. c3 ♘f6 7. ♖e1.

6... g6.

Or the plan ...e6 - ♘f6 - d5.

**7. c3 ♗g7 8. ♖d1 e5 9. ♘a3
♘ge7 10. d4.**

Instead of preparing it with 10. ♘c2, Fischer breaks in the center because he prefers open positions.

10... cxd4 11. cxd4 exd4.

11... ♘xd4 12. ♘xd4 exd4 13. ♘b5 ♘c6 is better.

12. ♘b5 0-0 13. ♘fxd4 d5.

Black takes hold of the center trying to get rid of his weak d-pawn.

14. ♘b3 a6 15. ♘c3 d4.

A superficial assessment would indicate that Black has solved his problems. The matter is deeper than that. Fischer's plan is to start an at-

tack over the dark squares starting on the queenside and creating threats to drive Black onto the defensive.

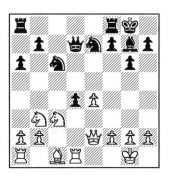

**16. ♘a4! ♖ae8 17. ♗f4! ♘d5
18. ♗g3 ♕e7.**

Black will try to get counterplay by attacking the e-pawn.

19. ♘ac5 ♔h8.

To prepare ...f5.

20. ♖e1.

Threatening 21. exd5 and trying to maintain the tension.

**20... ♘b6 21. ♖ac1 f5 22.
♕d2.**

White's pieces start to occupy all posts on the dark squares to prevent Black from operating on those squares, and so reducing their scope.

22... ♕f7 23. exf5 gxf5.

Ólafsson has played actively, accepting several weaknesses in return. Now he is threatening ...f4. Fischer's plan is to exchange as many pieces as possible to stress Black's weaknesses. Since this would not be enough, he combines this plan with an attack on the dark squares.

24. ♘d3 ♘d5 25. ♗d6.

(Note how the black pieces have to stay on the light squares).

25... ♖g8 26. ♘a5!.

The second plan: to exchange pieces to stress the weakness of the d4 and f5 squares.

26... ♘xa5.

26... ♘d8 is no solution due to 27. ♘e5.

27. ♖xe8 ♖xe8 28. ♕xa5.

In Fischer's games it is a recurring theme that he reaches many positions with the king- and queenside pawns on their initial squares. This is because he prefers open positions and to exert pressure with pieces alone.

28... h6 29. g3 ♔h7 30. ♘f4 ♘xf4.

White's threats are on the dark squares: ♖c7.

31. ♗xf4 ♕e6 32. ♗d2 ♖c8 33. ♖e1.

Always on the dark squares.

33... ♕f7?!.

Better 33... ♕g6.

34. ♖e7 ♕g6.

34... ♕xe7 35. ♕xf5† and 36. ♕xc8.

35. ♖xb7 f4.

The idea is …♕b1†.

36. ♕d5!.

Covering e4 and defending against all threats.

36... ♖e8?! 37. ♗xf4 ♖e1† 38. ♔g2 ♕d3 39. ♔h3 ♕g6 40. ♖d7! h5 41. ♔g2 h4 42. ♖d6! 1-0.

A dark-square symphony!

Miguel Najdorf—R. Fischer
Havana (Ol), 1966
A79

1. d4 ♘f6 2. c4 c5.

The Benoni. Fischer's main weapon has always been the King's Indian. From time to time he adopted the Grünfeld, the Nimzo-Indian, Benoni, and some variations of the Queen's Gambit.

3. d5 g6 4. ♘c3 ♗g7 5. e4 d6 6. ♘f3 0-0 7. ♗e2 e6 8. 0-0 exd5 9. cxd5 ♖e8.

Thematic: pressure on e4 to prevent e4-e5 with a real breakthrough.

10. ♘d2.

White's plans involve posting a Knight on c4 to exert pressure on d6, not allowing massive exchanges of pieces, maintaining the tension and trying to threaten Black as much as possible: attacking d6, threatening e5, or attacks on both flanks.

10... ♞a6 11. f3 ♞c7 12. a4 b6 13. ♔h1 ♞d7.

To answer White's ♞c4 with ... ♞e5. In the Benoni, Black must always be on the alert, but it also demands a great deal of "fending."

14. ♞c4 ♞e5 15. ♞e3 f5.

The Benoni also demands to be the first in attack if Black does not want to end up being kicked off the board. With the text, Black tries to de-activate White's threat of e5.

16. f4 ♞f7 17. exf5 gxf5 18. ♗d3 ♛f6 19. ♞e2.

White's plan is now to attack the f5-pawn.

19 ... ♞h6 20. ♞g3 ♛g6.

Preventing 21. ♞h5 because of 21... ♖xe3!.

21. ♛c2 ♖f8 27. ♗d2 ♗d7 23. ♖ae1?!

23. ♖f3 has been suggested as better.

23... ♖ae8 24. ♗e2?!

Here 24. ♗c3 is clearly better.

White is not aware of the fact that against Fischer all dilatory tactics are doomed to disaster.

24... ♖e7 25. ♗d3.

To prevent ... ♖fe8.

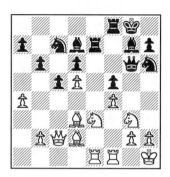

25... ♗d4!

Even in apparently closed positions the maintaining of positional tension, without losing time and without allowing your pieces to interfere with each other, is of paramount importance. Fischer has detected the key moment and is ready to carry out a positional transformation to convert his positional advantage into a permanent initiative. He manages to do this in his games because he is always thinking in terms of dynamism (always dealing with the creation of threats and the activation of his pieces, always fixing new targets for them and so forcing his opponents either to engage in active fights or to defend.) In this respect, it is very interesting to see his games against Petrosian, in the same way that it would have been very interesting to see how he would have played against a chess opponent like Karpov.

Why? Because both Petrosian and Karpov are experts at "drying up" the games.

26. b4 ♗xe3!!.

A very deep concept. The Bishop is exchanged for the Knight. It also begins a deeply-conceived plan which bears the mark of genius: to appreciate when standard rules can be discarded and allow the exceptions to take over.

27. ♗xe3 ♖fe8 28. bxc5 bxc5 29. ♗d2.

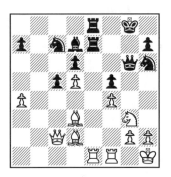

Najdorf cunningly sets a trap by offering his d5-pawn as bait. It is necessary to possess Fischer's degree of geniality to perceive all the nuances, and his tactical insight, to perceive all the possible intermediate moves. Fischer readily takes the pawn, withstands the ensuing attack and then manages to improve his superiority, stopping all of White's attempts. Tactically speaking, he is in command of the game. He seems able "to see" everything.

29... ♖xe1 30. ♖xe1 ♖xe1 31. ♗xe1 ♘xd5 32. ♗c4.

Here lies Najdorf's hopes. But Fischer had calculated that he could reorganize his pieces, creating threats.

32... ♕e6 33. ♗c3 ♗c6 34. ♕b3.

34. ♘h5 ♘g4 35. h3 ♘ge3.

34... ♔f7 35. ♕b8 ♘g8! 36. h3.

36. ♕xa7† ♘ge7 threatening ... ♕e3.

36... ♘ge7 37. ♕h8 ♕h6! 38. ♘e2 ♗xa4 39. ♕a8 ♗c6 40. ♕xa7 ♕e6 41. ♕a2 ♕e4!.

Threatening ♕xg2 after ♔g6 or ♔e8.

42. ♗d2 ♔e8 43. ♘g3 ♕d4† 44. ♔h2 ♘e3!.

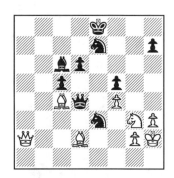

Forcing the exchange BxN due to the many threats to c4, f4 and g2.

45. ♗xe3 ♕xe3 46. ♗g8 ♕xf4 47. ♕f7† ♔d7 48. ♗xh7 ♗e4 49. ♗g6 ♕e5 50. ♗h5 ♗d5 51. ♕e8† ♔c7 52. ♔g1 ♕g7.

Threatening ...f4.

53. ♗d1.

Threatening ♗a4.

53... ♗c6! 0-1.

A typical game by Fischer with:

♙ Incisive opening play

♙ Maintaining (unrelenting) positional tension to obtain positional advantage always forcing the opponent.

♙ Transformation of the positional advantage into initiative.

♙ Acceptance of a tactical clash.

♙ Deep tactical insight.

♙ Unrelenting creation of threats.

In short, dynamic conception of chess at its best. Fischer seems always to be one step ahead of his rivals... or two!

Bobby Fischer
An Attempt at Analysis
Part 3

Positional Transformations:
Switching Advantages

Some authors have written here and there about this matter, saying that Fischer was a master at switching advantages, etc. Most of what has been written for over 30 years now reflects the truth, BUT lacks the necessary integrated vision. Fischer's craftsmanship at switching advantages and carrying out positional transformations is well-known. We can define the matter of positional transformations as the strategical alterations in the position in search of capitalizing on a positional advantage. It is an intrinsically dynamic process, since if it is not carried out, the opponent may be able to defend his position successfully. The process itself is made up of two different stages:

(1) the attainment of advantages;

(2) the transformation (very often through a heavy exchange of pieces, but also through an Exchange sacrifice) of the advantage (static) into a dynamic development. We are not speaking of combinative solutions although we have to admit that a combination is but a drastic example of transformation. Nevertheless, let's consider the matter in a purely stategical mode.

The ways in which the struggle may be transformed, as it has been said, are different but somehow standard. The point which reflects Fischer's craftsmanship and genius lies in two facts:

1. How he was able to obtain the advantage in his games, and

2. How he realized the key points of the game so as to carry out the process.

Fischer was able to steer his games into advantageous positions, thanks to different features: he knew the openings he used deeply after a profound analytical effort at home. This is why some of his victories came out immediately after the book moves where he had found a hole in his study.

On the other hand, his tactical insight, his strategical intuition, his machine-like way of calculating variations, and also his will to win, provided him with terrible weapons to use against all his rivals.

The perfect link between the process of getting the advantage and the precise timing to switch one advantage for another, so as to liquidate each position into a winning technical process by eliminating what was an accessory in a Capablancan fashion and jumping at the opponent in an Alekhinian way, is what turned him into a chess genius.

Books about Fischer are full of brilliancies: combinations, quick attacks, etc. Nevertheless, I would like to stress that in Fischer "all that glitters is not (only) tactics." If one wants to understand this genius, one must be ready to admit that Fischer was a perfect positional player too. The matter is that when confronted with such a chessplayer, most of his rivals were simply unable to understand his ideas and withstand the terrible strategical pressure on the board, and so commit mistakes that Bobby was ready to punish tactically.

Fischer was years ahead of most of his contemporaries, and perhaps only the Soviets with their enormous machinery working (for example, these are some of the names from that period: Smyslov, Tal, Petrosian, Spassky, Keres, Geller, Korchnoi, Stein, Botvinnik, Taimanov, Kotov, etc. And what about the Jugoslavs? Gligoric, Matanovic, Matulovic, and Ivkov. The Hungarians with Portisch on top, etc.) were the ones who could match, sometimes hamper, but had to give in at last, to Fischer.

How Can Fischer's Style Be Understood?

Fischer himself defined his chess style as "eclectic," that is, one that integrates the best characteristics from different and not always related sources. Let's labor a bit about all this.

Generally speaking, Fischer is regarded as a "classical" chessplayer. We have been using this word for many years and labelling with it the style of different players but I wonder what the meaning of it is. So we could try to define Fischer's style following a "negative path." Fischer is not a bizarre (Nimzovich-like) player. Fischer is not a speculative player (like Tal, for instance). Fischer is not like Réti, Spielmann, Lasker or Alekhine. In fact, Fischer is in a class by himself. His strategical approach to the game is that of Capablanca and Steinitz: subtle, smooth, unrelenting. But, Fischer developed himself as a player with the games, theoretical articles and influences of the so-called Soviet Chess School. He is a positional player with all the implications concerning the theoretical background. But Nature and work gave him the deadliest of weapons in the hands of a strategist: an overwhelming tactical (combinative and analytical) ability. Most annotators confronted with his tactical masterpieces forget that tactics in Fischer are but the peak of an enormous strategical iceberg.

In my opinion, Fischer was the first in developing the concept of dynamic strategy, for his style is dynamism in itself. He found new methods to deal with the problem of fighting for the initiative or defend actively, always keeping the game alive and burning. This has not been invented by Kasparov or Suba. In the matter of the openings, I am ready to accept that Kasparov is the best, but in the middlegame and all the processes involved, Fischer is light years ahead. Today's Russian trainers know a lot about it. But "Cold War" and "propaganda" had their own rules.

Fischer's Influences And A Psychological Approach

All chessplayers, even those who have been considered geniuses, have learned from their predecessors. They have their own preferred idols from the past and have extracted the best, blending all that with their modern approach to the game, so improving themselves and making chess advance with new ideas.

Several authors have written about Fischer's influences. As a genuine loner, he devoted all his energy to chess, creating a world of his own where nobody else could enter and damage him. He strove to depend only on himself, trying to dismiss any sort of chance, anything depending on good or bad luck. Fischer, simply, could not bear an imperfect and unjust world. He needed a perfect world and all he did was aimed at obtaining that goal. It is very easy to put adjectives before his name and smile in the belief that those who do not accept the world are "mad" while the sheepish crowd moving in a robot-like fashion, without ideas, are "right." I beg to differ... Fischer's "sin" was to keep himself aloof from an imperfect world trying to find his own way without accepting the hypocritical decrees of a cynical society. When a single individual does that, he is immediately labelled as "a loner," "mad," "unsociable," etc. The madding crowd will never accept one of its members becoming the voice of its conscience.

Fischer soon learned that when you laugh the world laughs with you, but that when you cry, you are left alone. He simply chose to be left alone from the beginning. He took refuge in chess (which is a whole universe in itself) and sought the self-affirmation of which he had lacked as a child. Chess was perfect: an absolutely just game where deception has no room, where only those who remain true to themselves and abide by its universal rules can get success. He made of it his one and only target.

All things considered, it is not difficult to understand why his main influences were Morphy, Steinitz, and Capablanca. Some authors have also mentioned Lasker, Alekhine and Nimzovich, but I do not agree (in an interview where he was asked about the ten best players, he did not bother to mention Lasker, among others). Of course, Fischer may have showed some minute characteristics from those players, but I think to Fischer's mind Nimzovich was too bizarre and indirect, Lasker too pragmatic[1], if not superficial. (We must not forget that Bobby only wanted to produce the very best move in every position, disregarding the facts of whom his opponent was, never adapting his play to the

[1] In a 1971 Denver Q&A Fischer admitted that Lasker should probably have been in his Top 10 List. Editor.

rival, always looking for the imposition of his own tempo and his own hallmark.) Alekhine was too speculative (a view shared by many others in spite of the Soviet hagiographic view of their chess giant).

So, from Steinitz, he learned the same he could have learned from Nimzovich but in a more scientific and pure way. From Morphy he learned the directness, alertness, and aggressiveness of the 19th century chess prodigy, and from Capablanca, the technical virtuosity and the crystal-clear way of formulating strategical concepts (apart from many other strategical and positional devices). Blend all this and you will have a formidable chessplayer, adding of course his own genius.

This is why in Fischer's games everything is smooth (Morphy, Capablanca), everything is scientific in both attack and defence (Steinitz), and everything has the precise components and the most economical means (Capablanca). Fischer was not perfect, no human being is, and competitive chess with a time limit is full of difficulties. But the most important thing is to realize that what really matters, what really makes us advance, is to accept that we can fight to get as near as possible to that ideal concept of "perfection." And the only way in which we can learn from those who have gone farther and further in that path is by understanding their virtues, avoiding their defects, and trying to imitate the good things in them, even learning from their mistakes.

Ultimate Approach

Apart from what has been said, there is still a question. Where does Bobby Fischer's secret lie? In my opinion, there are two distinct facts:

♟ His tactical insight that allowed him to calculate variations like a machine and within this his unsurpassed ability "to see" intermediate moves.

♟ His ability to provoke tactical situations where his pieces develop a series of different functions creating a minefield over the whole board in which the positions are full of occult tactical ambushes.

It must be explained that "tactical ambushes" flow naturally from the position due to different causes: election of active openings, dynamic interpretation of strategical motifs, tendency to fight for the initiative from the very opening, tendency to employ active devices when defending, never resorting to passive methods, etc.

All this implies an overwhelming degree of technical skill.

Fischer was able to become what he was because he devoted his entire life and his mind only to chess, in a part of the world where he had to fight alone and not always on the chessboard and against the Soviets.

Fischer's games are like the famous "Horn of Abundance" for they are full of tactical, strategical and technical subtleties.

With this article I would like to pay homage and show my gratitude to a man who devoted his life to chess, who taught me the secrets of chess and that with his example made most of us happier and wiser.

Final Considerations

1972 will remain forever as a sort of chess milestone. The Russians, that is, the Soviet School, had been dominating the chess world since 1948, winning tournaments, team events, chess olympiads, etc. The task was admirable: an enormous basis with children being taught chess at school and in the pride of the Soviet organization, the Pioneers' Palaces. Names like Botvinnik, Levenfish, Boleslavsky, Bondarevsky, Furman, Ragozin, Keres, Geller, Korchnoi, Kholmov, Stein, Polugaevsky, Taimanov, Bronstein, Smyslov, Tal, Kotov, Petrosian and so on. Against this whole machinery, a man alone... Robert James

Fischer.

After a lot of adventures starting in 1958 at the Portoroz Interzonal, he had reached the 1970 Palma de Mallorca Interzonal. He won it with 18½ points, 3½ points ahead of Larsen, Geller and Hübner.

His first rival in the Candidates Matches was Taimanov. When the dust of the battle settled and the smoke dispersed, the chess world could not believe it . . . +6 -0 =0 for Fischer. Taimanov and his seconds had underestimated Fischer, or perhaps they had not accurately assessed Bobby's strength. Larsen came next. The great optimist, one of the Western hopes (like Reshevsky, Gligoric, even Uhlmann). Unbelievably, another 6-0 for the American. This surpassed all expectations defying even the laws of logic. Petrosian was the last opponent and the only one who could provoke another match between the Soviets, thus keeping the previous title within Soviet borders. The pragmatic Petrosian had never been an easy rival for Fischer. Despite losing the first game, "Iron Tigran" stopped Fischer's victorious race, defeating him in the second game. The next three games ended in draws. Would Fischer fail again? Would the Soviets be, in fact, unbeatable? The last four games of the match dispelled any doubts: +4 -0 =0 for the American, with an overall result of +5 -1 =3. The road was clear.

After many difficulties, delays, negotiations and problems, the Spassky-Fischer match staged in Rejkjavik (Iceland) commenced. Spassky, a classical chessplayer who mastered all phases of the game, was a genuine representative of the Soviet Chess School. More books about this match have been written than about any other match. Fischer won by 12½ to 8½ (+7 -3 +11). What had happened? Apart from all the psychological warfare provoked by Fischer's exigencies, the second game awarded to Spassky after Fischer's refusal to play, etc., we could conclude that either the Russians, and Spassky himself, underestimated "the man alone," or the Soviets were laboring under the delusion that it could not be possible to defeat one Soviet player after another and reach the end by beating the last link, the Soviet World Champion. Some things seem clear: the Soviets mistakenly thought that Fischer was not going to be able to improve and excel himself and also be able to become a versatile chessplayer, changing at will his chess concepts and even his time-honored whole set of openings. Spassky even failed to appreciate some crucial points, and even thought that Fischer was inferior to him at assessing the key turning points in every game of chess. Spassky also thought that the American's style was too straight-forward and easy to predict.[2] The result was that Fischer imposed his technical skill in simple positions and when the Russian tried to complicate matters, he fell victim to Bobby's lethal tactical ability, which proved overwhelming. In the end, Fischer succeeded in achieving the one and only goal of his whole life. The world received the legacy of his genius manifested in his games.

After 1972, Fischer retired from chess and vanished, creating a legend. In 1992, he suddenly reappeared and played again against Spassky, but that is another story…

A few more games for your enjoyment.

Robert Byrne—R. Fischer
Sousse Interzonal, 1967
B87

A wild game with both sides creating and parrying threats. In the end, Fischer manages to impose his proverbial tactical ability always finding, time after time, the best of moves.

1. e4 c5 2. ♘f3 d6 3. d4 cxd4 4. ♘xd4 ♘f6 5. ♘c3 a6 6. ♗c4.

A spoonful of his own medicine: this was also Fischer's pet line as White. Byrne plays a psychological trump.

6… e6 7. ♗b3 b5 8. f4 ♗b7 9. f5 e5 10. ♘de2 ♘bd7 11. ♗g5 ♗e7 12. ♘g3 ♖c8 13. 0-0.

13. ♘h5!? would have been better. In this type of position, in which both sides are pursuing the initiative, one has always to choose the most forceful lines.

13… h5!.

Jumping at it: Fischer prevents all sorts of active plans on White's part based upon ♘h5 and starts his own attack on the kingside trying to force matters, driving the game into a blow-by-blow fight, setting himself the "tempo" of the struggle.

14. h4.

14. ♗xf6 ♘xf6 15. ♗d5 h4!.

14… b4 15. ♗xf6 ♗xf6! 16. ♘d5.

---

[2] In *Russians vs. Fischer,* Spassky, in a private strategy session with compatriots, was quoted as saying, "What do we do after Fischer slaughters us?" Spassky understood. Editor.

The key turning point. It is very important for a player to realize where the turning points of a game are: where he has to defend passively, start a counterattack, start an attack, provoke a massive exchange of pieces to make hidden factors appear, provoke a cramped position, etc. Fischer has allowed his rival to occupy d5 and has decided to keep his King in the center. Now he will have to show what he has planned to obtain in exchange. Deep calculation and tactical insight are called for.

16... ♗xh4 17. ♘xh5?!.

17. f6!? ♘xf6 18. ♘f5 ♗xd5 19. ♗xd5 0-0. Byrne accepts playing with fire.

17... ♕g5 18. f6! g6!.

Also good is 18... ♖xh5! 19. fxg7 ♖h7–+; equal is 18... ♕xh5? 19. fxg7; unclear is 18... ♘xf6 19. ♘hxf6† gxf6 20. ♘xf6†. 18... ♗xd5 is no solution since 19. fxg7 ♖g8 20. ♕xd5 is very dangerous.

19. ♘g7† ♔d8 20. ♖f3 ♗g3 21. ♕d3 ♗h2† 22. ♔f1 ♘c5 23. ♖h3?! ♖h4!!.

23... ♘xd3 24. ♖xh8† ♔d7 25. ♗a4† would give White some chances, though little hope. In any case, Fischer always chooses

(1) the most destructive blow,

(2) the most restrictive move for the opponent to prevent any sort of counterplay.

With the text Fischer also provokes a positional transformation of the tension (here it's threat against counterthreat) into a winning position, eliminating all traces of White's activity through a massive exchange of pieces.

24. ♕f3.

24. ♖xh4 ♕xh4 25. ♕f3 ♘xe4.

24... ♘xb3 25. axb3 ♖xh3 26. ♕xh3 ♗xd5 27. exd5 ♕xf6† 28. ♔e1 ♕f4 0-1.

Incidentally, here we have a recurrent feature in Fischer's approach to chess: it is typical of him NEVER to allow his pieces to interfere with each other. He is always looking for, if not creating, empty spaces for them.

Anthony Saidy—R. Fischer
U.S. Championship 1965-66
E45

♟ Prevention of counterplay reducing opponent's options.

♟ Deep tactical insight to detect all intermediate moves.

♟ Preventive thinking.

♟ Switching of advantages to reduce the opponent's options.

♟ Liquidation into an advantageous endgame.

♟ Use of the resource of the "ambush" as it is understood by problem composers.

1. c4 ♘f6 2. ♘c3 e6 3. d4 ♗b4 4. e3 b6.

Fischer's Variation in the Nimzo-Indian.

**5. ♘ge2 ♗a6 6. ♘g3 ♗xc3†
7. bxc3 d5 8. ♕f3.**

8. ♗a3 ♗xc4 9. ♗xc4 dxc4 10. 0-0 ♕d5 11. e4 ♕b5 12. ♕f3 ♘bd7 13. ♖fe1 is one of the modern possibilities too.

8... 0-0 9. e4.

9. cxd5.

9... dxc4!?.

In Portisch—Fischer, Santa Monica 1966, Fischer played 9... dxe4 and won a beautiful game in 35 moves.

10. ♗g5.

Threatening 11. e5.

10... h6 11. ♗d2?!.

11. h4 hxg5 12. hxg5 ♖e8 13. gxf6. But, perhaps 11... ♗b7.

11... ♘bd7 12. e5.

12. ♗e2.

12... ♘d5 13. ♘f5 exf5 14. ♕xd5.

White recovers the pawn by threatening both ♕c6 and ♕f3. But once again Fischer has the situation under control. This is a recurrent feature in Fischer's games, which I somehow associate with the concept of "ambush" as is used by problem composers. His opponents seem to have the best of both worlds when in fact they are about to fall between two stools.

14... ♖e8! 15. ♗xc4.

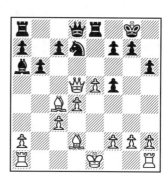

15. ♕f3 ♕c8 16. ♕xf5? ♘xe5; 15. ♕c6 ♘xe5 16. dxe5 ♖xe5† 17. ♗e2 ♕e8 18. ♕xe8 ♖axe8 19. ♗e3 f4; 15. 0-0-0 c5-+. Fischer is always able to parry threats, leaving his rivals with no counterplay after having enticed them into apparent activity.

15... ♘xe5!! 16. ♕xd8.

16. dxe5? ♕xd5 17. ♗xd5 ♖xe5-+.

**16... ♘xc4† 17. ♕xe8†
♖xe8† 18. ♔d1 ♘xd2 19. ♔xd2 ♖e2† 20. ♔c1.**

Fischer has sacrificed the Exchange for pawns and a more active position. Now comes the technical realization of his advantage (= initiative). This is the difference between Fischer and the rest. The initiative is something intangible, but in Fischer's hands it is like a battering ram.

20... ♖xf2 21. g3 ♗b7 22. ♖e1 ♗e4 23. ♖e3 ♖xh2 24. a4 h5 25. ♖a3 g5 26. ♖b3 f6! 27. a5

h4 28. gxh4 ♖xh4 29. ♖a3 ♖h7 30. axb6 axb6 31. ♖a7 ♖e7 32. d5 ♔f7 33. ♔d2 f4 34. ♖e1 f5! 35. c4 g4 36. ♖b7 g3 37. d6 cxd6 38. ♖xb6 f3 0-1.

♚

Mario Bertok—R. Fischer
Vinkovci 1968
A32

⚐ Overall perception and integrated vision.

⚐ Strategy + tactics / defense + attack.

⚐ Attack on the whole board reaching a multi-potential position with a variety of threats which forces the opponent to uncoordinate his pieces.

⚐ Liquidation into a superior endgame.

1. d4 ♘f6 2. ♘f3 c5 3. c4 cxd4 4. ♘xd4 e6 5. e3?!.
Too passive.

5... ♘c6 6. ♗e2 ♗b4† 7. ♗d2 ♗c5 8. ♘b3 ♗b6 9. ♘c3 d5 10. cxd5 exd5 11. ♘b5 0-0 12. 0-0 ♘e4 13. ♖c1 ♕g5! 14. ♗c3 ♖e8! 15. ♗d4.

Black threatened 15... ♘xf2. If 16. ♖xf2 ♕xe3 17. ♗d4 ♘xd4 18. ♘5xd4 ♖e4! 19. ♖c3 ♖xd4.

15... ♘xd4 16. ♘5xd4.
16. ♘3xd4 ♕e5=.
16... a5 17. ♗b5?!.

17. ♘f3!?; 17. a4 ♗h3 18. ♗f3 ♗d7 19. ♘b5? ♗xb5 20. axb5 ♘xf2—+.

17... ♗h3 18. ♕f3 ♗g4 19. h4.

19. ♕f4 ♕xf4 20. exf4 a4—+.

19...♕xh4 20. ♕f4 g5!.

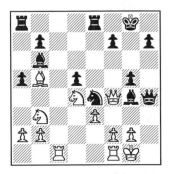

The famous "Fischer move!" It is not easy to explain why Fischer has always had a strong predilection for this move (both as White and as Black), but he has always seemed ready to use it as a sort of battering ram in key moments during his games, and not always with flying success. A psychological factor? Anyway here it does work, due to concrete aspects in the position.

21. ♕h2 ♕xh2 22. ♔xh2 ♖ed8 23. f3 a4 24. fxe4.

24. ♘a1 ♘d6 25. fxg4 ♗xd4 winning.

24... axb3 25. axb3 ♖a5 26. ♗d3 dxe4 27. ♗xe4 ♗xd4 28. exd4 ♖xd4.

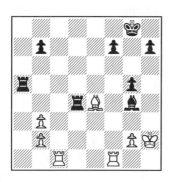

White is strategically lost.

29. ♗xb7 ♗e6 30. ♗c8 ♗xb3 31. ♖c3 ♖b5 32. ♖f2 ♖db4 33. ♗a6 ♖b6 34. ♗c8 ♔g7 35. ♗f5? ♖f6 36. ♔g1.

36. ♖cf3 ♗d5.

36... ♗e6 37. ♖cf3 ♖xf5 38. ♖xf5 ♗xf5 39. ♖xf5 ♔g6 40. ♖f2 h5 41. ♖c2 0-1.

41... h4 42. ♖f2 f5 43. ♖c2 g4 44. ♔h2 ♔g5 45. ♖d2 ♖e4.

R. Fischer—Gedeon Barcza
Stockholm 1962
B15

△ Positional attack.
△ Creation of weaknesses on different sectors of the board.
△ Deep calculation of variations always submitted to strategical plans.
△ Strategical masterpiece.
△ Pressure with pieces alone.
△ Switching of advantages; liquidation to better exploit the weaknesses.
△ Prevention of counterplay.
△ Maintenance of the positional tension.

1. e4 c6 2. ♘c3 d5 3. ♘f3 dxe4 4. ♘xe4 ♘f6 5. ♘xf6 exf6 6. d4 ♗d6 7. ♗c4 0-0 8. 0-0 ♖e8 9. ♗b3 ♘d7 10. ♘h4 ♘f8.

Fischer's concrete thinking is admirable. Black has to cover g6 from the threat ♕h5 and plans like c3-♗c2-♕d3.

11. ♕d3! ♗c7.

11... ♘g6 12. ♘xg6 hxg6, the f-pawn is pinned, 13. ♕xg6.

12. ♗e3 ♕e7.

12... ♕d6 13. f4 or g3.

13. ♘f5 ♕e4.

The key decision. Barcza resorts to radical methods to reduce White's activity in the belief that in a queenless positional game, he will be able to hold his position.

14. ♕xe4! ♖xe4 15. ♘g3 ♖e8 16 d5!!.

Starting a positional attack combined with piece pressure.

16... cxd5.

16... ♗b6?! 17. ♗xb6 axb6 18. ♖fe1 ♗d7 19. ♘e4 ±.

17. ♗xd5

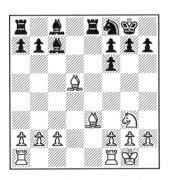

17... ♗b6?!

Creating a chronic weakness for himself. Annotators offer 17... ♘d7 18. b3± which then is no solution either. But what about 17... ♗e6 ? If 18. ♗xb7 ♖ab8 19. ♗e4 ♖xb2 20. ♗xa7 ♖xa2.

18. ♗xb6 axb6 19. a3 ♖a5 20. ♖ad1.

Activates the Rook, forces Black to fight for the central files to provoke a liquidation so as to exploit the weakened queenside, although it still will not be enough to win.

20... ♖c5 21. c3 ♖c7 22. ♗f3 ♖d7.

22... ♖e6 23. ♖d8.

23. ♖xd7 ♘xd7 24. ♘f5 ♘c5.

24... ♘e5 25. ♘d6 ♘xf3† 26. gxf3 ♖d8 27. ♘xc8 ♖xc8 28. ♖d1 ♔f8 29. ♖d7.

25. ♘d6.

Provoking Fischer's favorite endgame, a Bishop vs a Knight.

25... ♖d8 26. ♘xc8 ♖xc8 27. ♖d1!!.

Apparently 27. ♖e1 seems more logical, but what Fischer wants is

to prevent, firstly, any counterplay on Black's part, the d3 or a4 squares for the black Knight. A remarkable concept. White's Rook gets to the queenside anyway.

27... ♔f8 28. ♖d4.

28. ♖d6 ♘a4.

28... ♖c7 29. h3 f5.

29... ♔e7 30. ♖b4 ♘d7 31. ♗d5 and White's King marches over to the queenside, deciding the game.

30. ♖b4 ♘d7 31. ♔f1.

The King goes to the center and threatens to help in the attack on the queenside. Black's King hurries to help in the defense. So, to win the game, a second front will be necessary, two places to attack. Fischer will have to force matters on the kingside too. The game is very involved strategically: long-range strategical plans with short-range myriads of variations.

31... ♔e7 32. ♔e2 ♔d8 33. ♖b5! g6 34. ♔e3 ♔c8 35. ♔d4 ♔b8 36. ♔d5?!.

36. ♗d5 would be more accurate because it would start immediately

to touch Black's kingside to create weaknesses there.

36... ♖c6 37. ♔d4 ♖e6 38. a4 ♔c7 39. a5! ♖d6† 40. ♗d5!.

Fischer starts to attack the kingside following the positional principle of the "two weaknesses."

40... ♔c8.

40... ♘f6 41. axb6† ♔d7 42. ♔e5.

41. axb6 f6.

Or 41... ♘xb6 but Black is totally deprived of activity.

42. ♔e3 ♘xb6 43. ♗g8 ♔c7.

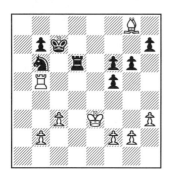

44. ♖c5†.

44. ♗xh7 is premature in view of 44... ♔c6 45. ♖b3 ♘c4† and ... ♖d2. Once again, Fischer stops his offensive to prevent his rival's counterplay. Instructive chess at its best!

44... ♔b8 45. ♗xh7 ♘d5† 46. ♔f3 ♘e7 47. h4 b6 48. ♖b5 ♔b7 49. h5 ♔a6 50. c4 gxh5 51. ♗xf5 ♖d4 52. b3 ♘c6.

52... ♘xf5 53. ♖xf5 ♖d3† 54. ♔e4 ♖xb3 55. ♖xh5 and ♖ to g6 winning.

53. ♔e3 ♖d8 54. ♗e4 ♘a5 55. ♗c2 h4 56. ♖h5 ♖e8† 57. ♔d2 ♖g8 58. ♖xh4 b5.

58... ♖xg2 59. ♖f4+–. Black desperately tries to reduce the number of weaknesses but Fischer holds a strong grip on the game, maintaining the positional tension with alternating attacks.

59. ♖f4 bxc4 60. bxc4 ♖xg2 61. ♖xf6† ♔a7 62. ♔c3 ♖g4 63. f4 ♘b7 64. ♔b4 1-0.

A masterpiece of positional chess, with Fischer dominating all areas of strategy and mounting an attack in an open position.

The following game will perhaps be unknown to most of you. It belongs to a session of simuls (20 boards) given in Madrid by Fischer. (At Madrid he received around £118, today's exchange rate, per session. Compare that with today's second-class IMs' fees!)

R. Fischer—García-Bachiller
Madrid 1970 (Simultaneous)
B43

1. e4 c5 2. ♘f3 e6 3. d4 cxd4 4. ♘xd4 a6 5. ♘c3 ♕c7 6. ♗d3 ♘f6 7. 0-0 b5 8. ♖e1 ♗b7 9. e5 ♘d5 10. ♘xd5 ♗xd5 11. a4! b4 12. ♗e4 ♗xe4 13. ♖xe4 ♘c6 14. ♗f4 ♖c8 15. ♖c1 ♕a7 16.

c3 bxc3 17. ♖xc3 ♗c5 18. ♗e3 0-0.

Is everything alright? Yes, for Fischer!

19. ♖xc5!! ♕xc5 20. ♘xe6! ♕a5 21. b4! ♘xb4 22. ♘xf8 ♘d5.

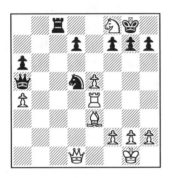

23. ♘xd7! ♘c3 24. ♕g4!!.

This was already seen by Fischer when he played 19. ♖xc5. Recall his ability to perceive intermediate moves both in attack and defense.

24... ♖c6 25. ♘f6† ♔h8 26. ♕xg7†! 1-0.

26... ♔xg7 27. ♖g4† ♔f8 28. ♖g8† ♔e7 29. ♖e8#.

BOBBY FISCHER—THE TROUBLED GENIUS

by Gudmundur G. Thorarinsson

When Bobby Fischer left Reykjavik after the Match in the autumn of 1972 he said to me that he was going to be a worthy world chess champion. He said he would participate in many tournaments and be much more active than the former champions thus furthering chess, trying to create a world-wide interest in the Royal Game. Reality turned out to be in complete contrast with these words. He isolated himself and did not play a single game publicly for 20 years.

For all chess enthusiasts the limelight had been on Bobby Fischer long before The World Chess Championship Match in Reykjavik 1972. His remarkable performances and results at an early age were unique. His character, strength of play and attitude towards organizers of chess events, and demands regarding conditions at chess tournaments and prize money, all this attracted attention, not only among chess players and people interested in chess but also among the general public in various countries throughout the world.

Outstanding results at the chessboard at a very early age and unbelievable results in tournaments and matches in the years before The World Chess Championship Match focused the attention of chess followers on Bobby Fischer.

The Match Of The Century

At the time of the match nearly everything added to the overwhelming interest that was focused on the event. In 1972 The Cold War was raging. The two superpowers were armed to the teeth and the theory of deterrence was believed to be the best ground for peace. The United States and The Soviet Union had divided the world into followers and enemies, the world was geographically divided into friendly and unfriendly countries and ideologically divided into capitalism and communism. Every dispute or conflict between these powers created unrest and worries amongst the people of the world.

Chess was the national sport of The Soviet Union. There the superiority of the Soviet Union at the chess board, the game of the minds, was regarded as an excellent advertisement for the superiority of the Soviet system over capitalism. The Soviet Union had dominated the chess world by winning nearly every international tournament both for individuals and teams and since 1948 no player outside The Soviet Union had reached high enough results to play in the final world chess championship match, i.e. for a quarter of a century. A world champion from another country seemed a distant dream.

In the United States chess was hardly known to the general public and was definitely not a high priority for the authorities. The interest in chess was not high in the country as a whole though they could pride themselves on many strong grandmasters.

The possibility of a competition for the world championship title in chess between representatives of the two main ideological systems, the two superpowers, in the world was exciting for nearly everyone. For the Soviet Union it was of imperial importance to defend their superiority in the chess field and for the United States it was an unexpected challenge to beat The Soviet Union at their own game. Therefore it was obvious that a match like that would arouse huge interest at even the highest level of governmental bodies in both countries.

In addition to this came the strange fact that the players were as unlike, as different in all aspects as possible. Their only common feature seemed to be that they were the two strongest chessplayers in the world. As men, as personalities, they were as different as day and night.

Boris Spassky came to Iceland nearly two weeks before the match was scheduled to start. They told me this was to adapt to the surroundings and the Soviet players were a little afraid of the light nights in Iceland, whether they would affect their sleep, even though Spassky coming from Leningrad, was not unfamiliar with such conditions. Spassky was a man of the world, he was relaxed, at least on the surface. An educated individual, his whole conduct was impeccable. He came from a country where chess was regarded with high respect and was indeed a national sport. An offspring of the famous Soviet School of Chess, he had been discovered at an early age, probably in school, for his unusual talent for chess and had been systematically trained. In that chess-loving country he had been given the best trainers, the best books, and participated in tournaments aimed at increasing his strength. And here he was, the World Chess Champion, having defeated the almost invincible Tigran Petrosian in a match for the world title, a national hero.

Bobby Fischer on the other hand came from a country where chess was not amongst the most popular sports. Even though the United States had several chess players of world class, chess was not among the top priorities there. The story goes that Bobby's father left his mother when young Bobby was only 2 years old and his mother had to support herself and her two children through life. She had to take work outside the home and she gave the 6 year old Bobby a chess set to occupy him while she was away from home. His sister taught him to move the pieces and there he sat on the floor alone moving wooden pieces from black squares to white ones. At the age of 14 he became the chess champion of The United States and soon became the strongest player of the country, above Reshevsky himself. In a total monomania he devoted his life to the goddess of chess. In an endless pursuit of perfection he sacrificed other values in life. It was said that he studied chess during the night playing music and slept during the day.

Thus while reaching the highest goal of the chessplayer, while digging into the core of the art of chess, he lost contact with the outer world to a large degree and did not adapt to the way of life led by the common man. He came forward with his stringent understanding of rules and regulations regarding the surroundings of chess tournaments, brightness of light over the chessboard, noise in the playing hall, the amount of prize money etc. His perception of righteousness did not allow for any compromises. He was feared by all organizers and at Sousse in Tunis he did not hesitate to leave in the middle of the tournament, even though he occupied first place, since his demands were not met. The Icelandic grandmaster Helgi Ólafsson has analyzed Fischer's style of playing and his evolution as a chess player. In an interesting lecture on the subject he came to the conclusion that the development of Fischer as a player could be divided into three phases. The first period from 1953 when he was at the age of about 10 to 1957. The next period from 1958 to 1966 and the last period from 1966 to 1972 when his unbelievable strength seemed overwhelming. The whole chess world cries over the lost games that were never played between 1972 and 1992.

His scores in the candidate matches before the world chess match were something no one had seen before, frightening for all chess players. He beat both Bent Larsen and Mark Taimanov six to zero and then followed an overwhelming victory over Tigran Petrosian. Chess fans thought they realised some resemblance to Stefan Zweig's *The Royal Game*. Something unexpected and unique was happening.

In view of all the surroundings, the cold war dominating world politics, the constant tension between the two superpowers, the superiority of the Soviet Union in the chessworld for decades, the isolation of this lone genius, people throughout the world sensed Fischer as one man against the system, as "the little man" standing alone confronting the superpower.

The Difference Between Knowledge And Intelligence

There is always a question what field of activity one should choose in life. Art is no doubt one of the most unquestionable values of life. Of all arts the art of living is probably the most important. Fischer did choose the art of the sixty four squares as his field of life. He once said, perhaps in a moment of weakness, "The only thing I can do is to play chess." Then, as a beam of joy came over his face he said: "But I do that very well."

In 1960 Fischer came to Iceland for the first time. He participated in a small tournament. There is an amusing story told from this his first visit to our country. His chessfriends in Iceland were showing him around in the city and as they drove along one of the main streets there was a hothouse to one side. There was a guidepost by the road pointing towards the hothouse with the name Alaska on it. The name of the hothouse was Alaska. When they drove by, the young genius turned his head and said: "So, that's the road to Alaska."

12 years later when Fischer came to Iceland to investigate the possible arena for his world chess championship, he told me he wanted to talk to the Icelandic grandmaster Fridrik Ólafsson. I gave him Olafsson's telephone number. Fischer did not find any satisfaction talking to me. He wanted to talk to someone who understood and mastered the mysteries of the royal game, one who said: if you play Bishop to a3, I simply play King to g7 and you gain nothing by Queen to c2 because of the Knight at f6 etc. The next day Fischer told me at the hotel that I had given him the wrong number. We argued for a moment and then he said: "Well a young woman came to the phone and she did not understand a word of English." Fridrik had a daughter 10 years old. Then to my amazement Fischer began repeating his conversation with the girl "She said something like 'Fridrik for ut,'" which means *Fridrik went out*. He repeated some sentences so that I could understand what the girl was saying. This was like a phonetic

Fischer and Leonid Stein from *Leonid Stein, Master of Risk Strategy*.

memory, as if he had recorded the conversation without understanding a word. This would be like a foreigner who, not being able to speak a word of Hebrew, calling Jerusalem, and though he got the wrong number the next day could repeat what some Jew had said in Hebrew on the phone so that other Jews could understand.

This was amazing. No doubt, Fischer could have been a scientist of world class, perhaps a Nobel prize winner in physics or chemistry if he had selected that path in life. His visual memory was as strong as his phonetic memory. And once you told him something he knew and remembered it verbatim. His devo-tion to chess, where he was challenged to the limits of his capacity, may have, for a period of time, restricted his interest in other fields of knowledge that you and I deem necessary, but his intelligence made them accessible for him when he found it worthwhile.

When he came to Iceland in February 1972 it was during the bi-annual International Reykjavik tournament. I took him to the playing hall. He rushed in and walked so fast that I had difficulty keeping up with him, took a short look at one of the inplay boards. I recall that it was the Soviet grandmaster Stein playing the British international master Keene. He immediately declared: "Stein is

R. Keene—L. Stein
Reykjavik International 1972
GRÜNFELD DEFENCE D91
notes by Bragi Kristjánsson

1. d4 Nf6 2. c4 g6 3. Nc3 d5 4. Bg5 Ne4 5. Bh4 Nxc3 6. bxc3 Bg7 7. e3 c5 8. cxd5 Qxd5 9. Nf3 Nc6 10. Be2 cxd4 11. exd4 (11. cxd4) **Qa5?!** (11... e5!) **12. 0–0 Qxc3?!**.

13. Rc1 Qb4 14. Rb1 Qd6 15. Bg3 e5 (15... Qd5 16. Rb5 Qxa2 17. d5 Nb8 18. d6 0-0 19. dxe7 Re8 20. Ne5! Bxe5 21. Bxe5 Nc6 22. Ba1 Qe6 23. Qd2 f6 24. Rd5 Qxe7 25. Bc4 Be6 26. Rd7 Qc5 27. Qh6 1-0, Keene—Eales, British Championship 1971. **16. Nxe5 Qxd4.**

This is the position Fischer was watching. The players agreed to a draw, but Fischer saw immediately that Stein was lost. The following analysis seems to prove him right:

17. Nxc6 bxc6 18. Bd6 Be6 19. Rb7 Qxd1 20. Rxd1.

Now Black has three possible ways of defending:

a) 20... Bf8 21. Be5 Rg8 22. Bf6 Bg7 23. Rxa7 Rb8 24. Bxg7 Rxg7 25. Bf3 c5 26. a4 Rc8 27. Re1 Kf8 28. a5 c4 29. a6 c3 30. Bb7 Rc7 31. Ra8† Ke7 32. a7 c2 33. Re8† Kxe8 34. a8=Q† and White wins.

b) 20... Bf6 21. Bf3 Bd5 22. Bxd5 cxd5 23. Re1† Kd8 24. Rxf7 Bc3 25. Bc7† Kc8 26. Rc1 d4 27. Ba5 Re8 28. Rc7† Kd8 29. Rxa7† Bxa5 30. Rxa8† Kd7 31. Rxa5 and wins.

c) 20... Bd5 21. Bf3! Bxf3 22. Re7† Kd8 23. gxf3 Bh6 24. Rxf7 and Black is completely helpless, e.g. 24... Bg5 25. Bc5† Ke8 26. Rb7 a5 27. Bb6 Bf6 28. Rd6 Ba1 29. a4 Rc8 30. Bc5 Ra8 31. Re6† Kd8 32. Rxc6 g5 33. Kg2 Ke8 34. Re6† Kd8 35. Ree7 Kc8 36. Rec7† Kd8 37. Be7† Ke8 38. Bxg5 Rg8 39. Re7† Kf8 40. Rf7† Ke8 41. Rbe7† Kd8 42. Re5† Kc8 43. Rc5† Kb8 44. Rxh7 etc.

completely lost." At the same moment there came up a sign. The players had agreed on a draw. Fischer shook his head, lost his interest in the tournament and walked out. The next day on our way to the airport I asked him whether he was sure that Stein had a lost game. He took from his pocket a chess set, and with quick movements put up the position which he had in his mind, although he had only glimpsed it for a second the day before and showed me several possible variations and said: "Completely lost. There is nothing he can do." The two grandmasters had been playing, studying the game over the board for two or three hours and agreed on a draw. It took Fischer only a split second to realize that Stein had a completely lost game.

Match Of The Century Again

I always thought that this was too ambitious a name for the event. But some of us believed this was really the right name and others thought that this name was good for increasing interest in the match. Now 30 years later people are coming to Iceland, interviewing those who were involved in the match, making films and writing books about the match. So maybe I was wrong, maybe this was the Match of the Century.

Here is neither the right time nor the place to discuss the tumultuous times of preparation, negotiation and organizing, or the incredible match itself. The individuals involved, the players who were the towering figures of the chess world were highly intelligent, highly disciplined hard workers with supreme self-confidence and had in life been driven by a dream and love for the game of chess. The public was spellbound by this event. When I try to recall this time 30 years later, somehow the difficulties of this ordeal fly like a firebrand through my mind. As the old saying goes: "It is the brightest hours that fade away the fastest."

Looking back it seems like foolhardiness to continue after the Yugoslavs gave in.

I was very reluctant to have The Icelandic Chess Federation participating in the open tender FIDE had prepared for the match. I thought that the possibilities that Iceland would in the end host the match were close to zero. It was more under pressure from my colleagues that I agreed to go along. Spassky's choice to put Iceland number one turned the course of events. And suddenly we were in the turmoil of the whole negotiation although we only had the third highest bid.

The complex and difficult twists around conditions included prize money, gate money, time of sunset on Fridays in Iceland at the beginning of Sabbath, the selection of chess sets and boards, and the preparation of the playing hall. Then the challenger did not show up for the opening ceremony nor for the first game. This resulted in complex disputes and negotiations about the televising and photographing in the hall during the match, the chair, and the lighting incident. Then with Fischer losing the second game by forfeit the Soviet Chess Federation wanted to call Spassky home because they felt the world chess champion had been humiliated in Iceland, and so on.

To save the match at its start seemed an unsurmountable task. We were really afraid that here was a tragedy in the making. Many of our co-operators were doing all in their power but at times everything seemed in vain. It was like ordering the tide not to come in. I could mention the British financial giant, James Slater, who doubled the prize money, Dr. Max Euwe, president of FIDE, who fought fiercely to bring the match to reality, Lothar Schmidt the chief arbiter who often found a path where there was no path before, Fridrik Ólafsson who contributed in many ways to help and the board of The Icelandic Chess Federation who had the main burden on its shoulders. Was it Spassky, or Saemundur Palsson, Bobby Fischer's friend and bodyguard, who saved the match?

Strangely enough, looking back, trying to weigh everything that happened, I feel convinced that *The Match of The Century* was saved by a misunderstanding. After a thorough and difficult preparation and organization it is hard to admit that it was not the planning nor the calculations of the Icelandic Chess Federation that saved the match, it was simply a misunderstanding. Somehow I have the feeling that now after 30 years the Match is living its own life. It does not need any explanations from me or others from the organizing team. People see the Match from different directions than we did. Time is outlining and underlining perspectives that we did not grasp in the heat of the close combat. The Match has grown old enough to take care of itself.

A Peculiar Incident,
A Misunderstanding

Fischer had not arrived in Iceland at the time of the opening ceremony. He was not present when the first game was to start according to the schedule. The organizers had already invested a lot of money in the preparations and everyone was interested in this event, which the whole world followed closely, taking place. The Icelandic Chess Federation who had been swallowing many bitter pills, tried to come to grips with the problems. It was not difficult to gauge the public mood, it was close to panic. One of the ideas that were put forward was to try to convince Spassky to talk with Fischer, to try to break the spiral of the incessant dispute. Spassky was interested in playing the match. He was confident, and he had never lost to Fischer. Perhaps he was also interested in the prize money. Spassky was willing to talk to Fischer if Fischer phoned him but he was not willing to make the phone call himself. It was not possible to reach Fischer to persuade him to phone Spassky. We were therefore even discussing the possibility of connecting their phones without either of them actually making the call. We were convinced that such a "tete-tete" might help. The two players had a friendly attitude towards each other but all the fuss in the media, the lawyers and the negotiators was making waves. While we were playing with this idea the phone rang. Spassky was on the line. He wanted to talk. We agreed to meet in a Reykjavik hotel. Geller, Krogius and Nei accompanied him but our talk was private. Spassky told me that the situation was getting serious and it was out of his hands, this had to be solved at a higher level. With my mind totally occupied with the problem that the challenger had not arrived, I had not thought of that possibility. In a flash I replied:" If the

matter can be solved at a higher level, that will be done."

I went immediately to see the Prime Minister of Iceland, Olafur Johannesson and told him that our opinion was that our dilemma could be solved by an official request from the government of Iceland to the White House, asking the government to apply pressure in the matter. The Prime Minister had followed the preparations and was well informed of the present situation. At first he did not believe in this solution, but after some discussion he agreed to give it a try. He requested to see the U.S. Ambassador. It so happened that the Ambassador was not in Iceland at the time but the *chargé d'affaires* came in his place. The Prime Minister explained that Iceland had done everything in its power to make this match a reality. It seemed that the behavior of the American grandmaster was creating a hostile atmosphere towards the U.S. and he asked the *chargé d'affaires* to consider if the embassy could use its influence to ease things to a positive solution.

At the final ceremony the *chargé d'affaires* told me that he had hurried to the embassy and called the White House expressing an official request from Iceland that the U.S. government intervene in this matter.

One of Fischer's lawyers later

told me that he had been trying in vain to persuade Fischer to go to Iceland to play the match when the phone rang. On the line was Secretary of State, Henry Kissinger. Kissinger had asked Fischer to go to Iceland and play Spassky, and said that the American nation expected him to beat the Russian.

The lawyer said that Fischer's expression changed completely. He looked like a soldier going to war, his attitude was different. He declared that he would go to Iceland and play. When he was asked why he had changed his mind so suddenly he is supposed to have replied "I have made up my mind that the interest of my nation is above my own." So Fischer left for Iceland on the next plane.

Of course I was immensely relieved. When I met Spassky, after Fischer had arrived and I was going to thank him for his good advice he said worriedly: "Gudmundur, you have done nothing in spite of what you promised me." It was like a light bulb over my head. Immediately I understood the situation. The Soviet authorities were getting very displeased with the proceedings. They felt that the World Champion was being humiliated by the way things had turned out since he arrived in Iceland. They wanted to call him back and refuse to play. With all my attention focused on the problem of

Fischer's absence I had overlooked what was happening on the Soviet side and their possible reaction. I looked Spassky in the eyes and said: "I will meet with the Prime Minister today to discuss the situation."

Again I went to the Prime Minister and informed him about my conversation with Spassky. The Prime Minister requested to see the Soviet Ambassador and told him of the Icelandic people's admiration and sympathy for Spassky and expressed the hope that with the kind co-operation of the Soviet authorities the match might still take place in spite of the challenger's behavior. The Ambassador communicated with his authorities and a little later a message

announced that Spassky would play, albeit "under protest."

So at last the match could start though many obstacles were to rise which could jeopardize the event.

The main point is that I misunderstood Spassky. I was so preoccupied with the problem of Fischer's absence and his problems that I had only partly understood what was going on. The conversation with Spassky started an operation which saved the match. In reality things were so complex that the match had to be saved many times by different interventions from different parties. But this time the match was saved by pure misunderstanding and I am convinced that without it there would have been no match.

A Self-imposed Exile

For 20 years Fischer did not play one single public game. When the 10 years' anniversary of the match in Reykjavik was approaching the Icelanders were interested in inviting Fischer to Iceland thus commemorating the great chess event. From Joan Targ, Fischer's sister and her husband, we got the information that we could contact Fischer through Claudia Mokorow in Pasadena, California. She gave us some good advice and we sent a letter to Fischer at her address. We were to give him our phone number in the letter and he was supposed to ring

collect, which he never did. We offered him three possibilities, to play a match against an Icelandic grandmaster, to play in a tournament with 5 Icelandic grandmasters, or come as a guest of honour to the 10 years' anniversary of The Match. It was interesting that Claudia told us Fischer had actually been negotiating with many people about returning to the chess board. She said he had on several occasions been travelling with the aim of concluding these negotiations but these people seemed more interested in advertising themselves, showing that they had contact with Fischer, than finalizing contracts. Therefore he would not be available for more negotiating travels now.

We were told that it was essential to address him as World Chess Champion as he had never lost the title and a considerable sum of prize money was important. Claudia said Fischer was not playing chess but he studied a lot. We had also heard of a letter that Fischer had written to the President of FIDE, Campomanes, where he expressed his will to play but said: "There has to be money at every step of the way."

In short, every attempt to get Fischer to the board had been in vain for 20 years.

The Troubled Genius
But on the 20th anniversary of

The Match, Fischer played a rematch with Boris Spassky in Sveti Stefan in Yugoslavia. The rematch showed that he had preserved his strength to a remarkable degree. At that time the U.S. government had prohibited every U.S. person from making any contract in support of a commercial project in Yugoslavia as well as exporting services to Yugoslavia. The U.S. government had imposed sanctions against Serbia and Montenegro. "Aye, there's the rub." The Office of Foreign Assets Control deemed Fischer's participation in the rematch to be in support of the sponsors' commercial activities. His participation was regarded punishable by public penalties not to exceed $10,000 or 10 years in prison or both. The rematch attracted attention throughout the world but now the interest was not due to the cold war or the tension between the superpowers. It was the person Robert Fischer, who once again created worldwide interest in chess and this chess event. In the words of columnist Charles Krauthammer writing for *Time Magazine* this was the greatest comeback since Napoleon Bonaparte sailed a single masted fleet from the island of Elba in the year 1815.

The self imposed exile turned into an exile by law. Since 1992, for 10 years, Fischer has not been able to visit his native country. During this time his closest relatives, his mother and his sister, have died and he was not able to attend their funerals. A storage room which he had rented in Pasadena was broken up and all his belongings confiscated and auctioned for a trifling debt of around $400. Apparently he had made attempts to pay the debt without results, having no contacts.

The man who brought the World Chess Champion title single handedly to the U.S. and was hailed together with the swimmer Mark Spitz as a national hero has now been an international fugitive for 10 years. Completely isolated, this lone genius has no access to his home country, and is broken off from friends and relatives. One of the biggest names in the chess world, who devoted his entire life to moving wooden pieces from white squares to black squares in a demonic monomania and never has hurt a fly, except perhaps with his harsh words, is a listed and wanted criminal. Why? For playing chess in a country where the U.S. government has prohibited U.S. persons to participate in commercial projects. Bobby Fischer is no threat to either world peace or world business. Stalin once asked: "How many divisions has the Pope?"

Recently several of Fischer's chessfriends in Iceland requested a meeting with the American Ambassador in Reykjavik and asked her to look into the matter of her countryman, Robert Fischer, World Chess Champion 1972-1975. By bringing the case to the attention of the Ambassador they hoped to have the case against the troubled genius dropped. This was in vain. According to the Ambassador no one can open Fischer's case except Fischer himself or someone per signed procuration from Fischer. That would probably not be easy to get.

No surprise that these 10 years of exile have affected his mental strength and focused his mind against the United States. The historians of the future will not find it easy to understand the conduct of the U.S. Before our very eyes we have a personal tragedy. Will the future not judge the U.S. severely and without sympathy?

Is there is something rotten in the State of the dollar?

Preparations For The Match

When someone first mentioned the idea that Iceland should participate in the open bid for the world chess championship, I just shook my head. I immediately judged it as nonsense. I thought larger countries would offer a far larger prize fund and would have such an advantage, that sending an offer would only be a waste of time. At the last moment though, the board of the Icelandic Chess Federation decided to participate. With the third highest offer we unexpectedly stood in the limelight as one of the potential organizers. The run-up to the championship was an enervating affair. FIDE decided to stage the match in two parts in two countries. The negotiations with the Yugoslavs took a lot of time and a lot of energy. In the turmoil of unexpected incidents and an uncertain future the Yugoslavs withdrew and Iceland took over the task of staging the whole match. At that time Dr. Euwe had been looking for an organizer of the first half for several days. No country was willing to take the risk. **Now, looking back one can speculate what would have happened if Iceland had withdrawn?** An interesting question which will never be answered.

The uncertainty surrounding the whole event put us in severe time pressure. It was our responsibility to secure excellent playing conditions, the proper playing hall, sufficient and convenient lighting, etc. For a large part of the preparation time we were negotiating agreements concerning television and photography rights. For most of the preparation time no one was sure whether there would be a match. Working under such conditions is difficult to say the least.

A special playing table was designed and around twenty different chess boards were made, from which Fischer could choose. Boris Spassky simply said: "I leave these things to Fischer, if he is satisfied I have no objections." The chess boards were both made of stone and wood. The first game was played on a stone board but then we changed to wood. There was a large discussion on the size of the squares and the contrast of the colors between the white and the black squares on the one hand and between the black and white pieces, and, the squares on the other. The ICF had built a large lighthelm covering the whole stage with a dimmer so the strength of the brightness could be continuously changed from darkness to such a brightness that one could hardly stand to be on the stage. Contrary to previous tournaments that Fischer had played in there were no complaints about the light. The seats of the audience had to be moved to such a distance that noise would not disturb the players. We designed a large screen on which we showed each game, move by move, using electronics, which was rather unusual at that time. The players had separate rooms behind the playing stage to which they could withdraw if they wished to do so. Each player had at his disposal a suite at a hotel. No complaints were raised regarding these material surroundings, but disputes continued as to television and photography rights, and questions were raised regarding possible disturbances from chairs and stage surroundings as people became familiar with them during the match.

Reykjavik
August 2002

MY GAME WITH FISCHER
1964

by Mike Morris

In the summer of my 14th year I stepped into the Mechanics' Institute Chess Room for the first time. This venerable San Francisco institution is the oldest chess club in the West. Along the walls were photos of past events at the club; prominent was one of Capablanca giving a simul in 1916. The same wooden chess sets shown in the picture were on the tables, more than a little worn from hard play over the years.

I was greeted by Arthur B. Stamer, the club's director. His picture was also on the wall playing in a radio match in the 1920's. He told me to play him to determine my starting rating on the club's rating board. Even though he was still expert strength I held him to a draw and he gave me a position midway on the board. I was quite proud.

The chess club was actually overseen by Charles Bagby, a member of the Board of Trustees of the Mechanics' Institute. Bagby was a pompous and portly lawyer with a raspy voice and a tyrannical manner. I heard that Bobby Fischer was going on tour and I asked Bagby whether the club would be bringing him to San Francisco. Bagby asked how much money Fischer expected and I told him $500 for his appearance. Bagby responded, "Tell Fischer that he can [expletive deleted]." This came not only as a shock to my young (16 years old) ears but also as a disappointment that our club would be bypassed.

Apparently more influential club members prevailed on Bagby to bring Fischer, and his simul was scheduled for April 13, 1964. Fischer opened with a lecture on one of his recent games and then proceeded to play 50 boards. Our club had the best record of the tour. We won 4 and drew 8, as I recall. I definitely remember the sensation being Robert Burger's victory with the Fritz variation of the Two Knight's Defense. It was the first time I ever heard of the variation and the last time I have ever seen it played. Incidentally, this game was published in Larry Evans' column in the August 1999 *Chess Life*.

Fischer played rapidly except when he stopped at the board next to me, occupied by a boy about 11 years old. Then he would look at the kid for a while before moving. I think Fischer saw something of himself in the youngster and was contemplating his own lost childhood.

Even though a piece up, Fischer offered me a draw after 46 moves because he could make no progress. I asked Bobby to autograph my scoresheet, and he signed it as I handed it to him, that is, upside down on the page.

Mr. Stamer died shortly before the event and in May the club held the first A. B. Stamer Memorial tournament. My rating was 1863 but I beat a strong expert and an A player, drew two other experts and I lost only to Robert Burger. I didn't mind—I was in good company. The combination of these two successes hooked me on chess for life and provided enough momentum to overcome all the unsound combinations, time pressure blunders and lost opportunities that I have encountered since.

R. Fischer—Michael Morris
San Francisco (simul), April 1964
FRENCH RUBINSTEIN C10

[Donaldson and Tangborn]

1.	e4	e6
2.	d4	d5
3.	Nc3	dxe4
4.	Nxe4	Nd7
5.	Nf3	Ngf6
6.	Nxf6†	Nxf6
7.	Bd3	b6
8.	0-0	Bb7
9.	Qe2	Be7
10.	Rd1	0-0
11.	c4	Qe8

Black wants to play ...c5, but needs to get his Queen off the d-file. Besides the text, another way to prepare ...c5, though in fact it was never played in the game, is 11... Qc8; 12. Bg5 h6 13. Bd2 Re8 14. b4 a5 15. b5 c6 16. bxc6 Qxc6 17. Rab1 Rab8 18. Bf4 Bd6 19. Bxd6 Qxd6 20. Ne5 Nd7 21. Qe3= *Psakhis—Akopian, Halhidiki 1992*.

12.	b3	c5
13.	Bb2	Rd8
14.	dxc5	Bxc5
15.	a3	

GM Reshevsky used the plan of 15. Bxf6 gxf6 16. Be4 in an analogous position to try to steer for a better ending.

15.	...	Qc6
16.	b4	Bd6
17.	Rac1	

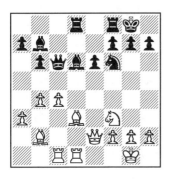

17. ...   Rd7??

Morris overlooks a tactic. Better was 17... Bf4 with complicated play.

18. c5!

Black has no good answer to the threats of 19. b5 or 19. Bb5.

18. ...   Bb8
19. Bb5?

Simply 19. b5, followed in most cases by 20. c6, winning material.

19. ...   Rxd1†
20. Rxd1   Qc7
21. cxb6

21. c6 Bxc6 22. Rc1 Bxb5.

21. ...   axb6
22. h3

22. Ne5 looks better.

22. ...   Rd8

22... Bxf3 23. Qxf3 Qh2† 24. Kf1 Nd5 threatens ...Nf4. White may be forced to meet this move with g3 pitching the h3 pawn, but seeking compensation in the Bishop pair, d-file and Black's offside pieces.

23. Rxd8†   Qxd8
24. Bd3   Qd5
25. Bc4   Qf5
26. Qd3   Qxd3

27. Bxd3   Nd5
28. Bd4   Nf4
29. Bf1

It might look illogical to surrender the Bishop pair when the opponent had a queenside majority, but 29... Bxf3 makes some sense as after 30. gxf3 the white King has a hard time becoming active.

29. ...   Nxh3†
30. gxh3   Bxf3
31. Bxb6   Bd6

Morris stops Bobby from activating his majority with 32. a4.

32. Bg2

32. ...   Bxg2

A difficult decision as 32... Bd1 makes it hard for White to activate his queenside pawns.

33. Kxg2   Kf8
34. a4

White can go into a pawn endgame with 34. Bc5 but after 34... Bxc5 35. bxc5 Ke7 36. a4 Kd7 37. a5 Kc6 38. a6 g5 it's hard for him to break through. The best try might be 34. Kf3 bringing the King up the board to support the queenside pawns with the Bishops on the board.

34.	...	Bxb4
35.	a5	Bxa5
36.	Bxa5	f6

The reduced material guarantees that sensible play will draw for Black.

37.	Kf3	Kf7
38.	Ke4	Kg6
39.	Bb4	Kf7
40.	Kd4	Kg6
41.	Bd6	Kf5
42.	Bf8	g5
43.	Be7	Kg6
44.	Kc5	h5
45.	Kd4	Kf5
46.	Ke3	

The game was drawn.

MEETING BOBBY FISCHER

by Grandmaster Wolfgang Unzicker

A chapter from *Schachphänomen Bobby Fischer* by Alexander Pasternjak reprinted with permission from Edition Olms 1991. Translated from the original German by FM Bragi Kristjánsson.

At the grand international tournament in Buenos Aires 1960 I was going to meet Robert Fischer for the second time. As in all great tournaments, there was no shortage of predictions as to the outcome of the tournament.

I can still remember very well how a member of the organizing committee gave the opinion, which was widely accepted, that the tournament would not be won by the Russians, it would either be won by Fischer or Gligoric.

As so often happens, the prophets were also wrong this time. Both the proclaimed favorites were in miserable form almost during the whole tournament. This was especially the case with Fischer who at times was unrecognizable. As was the case in Zürich I also met him in the middle of the tournament in Buenos Aires. This time I had the white pieces and Fischer played the Sicilian Defense as he often did. Fischer played the opening in a quiet and safe, but also rather unusual way. Suddenly, I could not believe my eyes, Fischer, on the move, firmly picked up the h-pawn, obviously to move it. A few seconds later his hand let go of it.

In a book, I am not going to give it's title, the story is told, that Fischer, deep in thought, had been playing with the h-pawn and realized, to his agony, that it was on the chessboard, but not beside it. As is the case with many affirmations given on this game I must send this one into exile in the kingdom of legends.

With my 20 years of tournament praxis I can see the difference between a player absent-mindedly just playing with the piece and a player really grabbing the piece with the intention of moving it.

In this moment Fischer showed exemplary fairness. Having picked up the pawn he moved it, by the rule: touch-move, even though it was the losing move for him. I had not intended to protest if Fischer had in fact made a move with another piece. It would have been difficult for me to prove that he had broken the touch-move rule, besides I do not at all like to turn to the arbiters in cases like these.

Fischer lost this game because of a momentary oversight and his fairness and this win has never given me any pleasure.

W. Unzicker—R. Fischer
Buenos Aires 1960
SICILIAN DEFENSE B98

1.	e4	c5
2.	Nf3	d6
3.	d4	cxd4
4.	Nxd4	Nf6
5.	Nc3	a6
6.	Bg5	e6
7.	f4	Be7
8.	Qf3	Qc7
9.	0-0-0	0-0
10.	Bd3	Nc6
11.	Nxc6	bxc6
12.	Qg3	

14.	fxe5	Ng4
15.	Bxe7	Qxe7
16.	Ne4	Qc7
17.	h3	Nxe5
18.	Nf6†	Kh8
19.	Qg5	Nxd3†
20.	Rxd3	gxf6
21.	Qxh5†	Kg7
22.	Qg4†	1-0

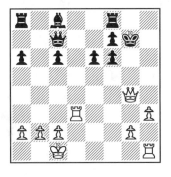

12.	...	h5?
13.	e5	dxe5

BOBBY FISCHER IN EUROPE AND IN PRINT

by FM Bragi Kristjánsson

In Reykjavik in 1960

Fischer came to Reykjavik, Iceland, on the 30th of September, 1960 to take part in an international tournament held in the memory of Eggert Gilfer, the grand old man of Icelandic chess, who had passed away earlier that year. For some reason Fischer arrived too late for the Gilfer Memorial, which ended on the 1st of October. The Icelandic Chess Federation arranged a small tournament of five players for the 5th-10th of October. Besides Fischer, GM Fridrik Ólafsson, Ingi R. Jóhannsson, later IM, who won the Gilfer Memorial, Freysteinn Thorbergsson, 1960 Champion of Iceland, and Arinbjörn Gudmundsson, third at the Gilfer Memorial, played in the event.

The tournament was won by Fischer, scoring 3.5 points of 4, the draw being against Thorbergsson, and his game with Gudmundsson found its way into Fischer's classic book, *My 60 Memorable Games,* nine years later. The placing of the others: 2. Jóhannsson, 2.5 points, 3. GM Ólafsson, 2 points, 4-5. Thorbergsson and Gudmundsson, 1 point each.

On the 2nd of October there was a blitz-tournament (5-minute games), 6 players, double round robin. The result was:

1. Robert Fischer, 8.5 points (a loss to Ólafsson, draw with Ásmundsson),
2-3. GM Ólafsson, IM Svein Jóhannessen (Norway), 7 points each,
4. Ingvar Ásmundsson, 4 points (Blitz Champion of Iceland 1960, Champion of Iceland 1979),
5. Gudmundur Ágústsson (one of the best players in Iceland for many years, represented Iceland at the Chess Olympiad in Amsterdam 1954), 2 points.

6. Gudmundur S. Gudmundsson (Icelandic Champion 1954, played at the Amsterdam Olympiad 1954, 3rd at Hastings 1946/47), 1 point.

Fischer did not seem to be in high spirits during his stay in Iceland, at least that was the description of the reporters he spoke to. He was in difficulties in his tournament games against Ólafsson and Jóhannsson, but scored fighting wins in both games. Two and one half months earlier he had played in the only really bad tournament of his life, the 1960 Buenos Aires International.

In Cøpenhagen in 1962

Fischer visited Cøpenhagen on his way back from his great triumph in the Stockholm Interzonal. He stayed there from 9-11 March, 1962 as the guest of the Cøpenhagen Chess Federation. This visit had been planned during Fischer's one day stay in Cøpenhagen on his way back from the Alekhine Memorial in Bled the year before. Fischer had promised to participate in two chess arrangements in Cøpenhagen on this occasion. His pay would only be $600, luckily for the Danes it had been agreed upon the year before the Interzonal.

On his arrival in Cøpenhagen on Friday, the 9th of March, which by the way was on Fischer's 19th birthday, he was invited to the American embassy for a half hour meeting with the ambassador, Mr. MacCormick Jr.

In the evening he played a game behind locked doors with GM Bent Larsen, lasting from 7 p.m. to midnight, with Fischer playing black and winning the game. It was broadcast over the Danish radio the following day with the comments of the two grandmasters. It was also shown the same day on Danish television, the first whole game of chess to be televised in Denmark and if we are to believe the Danes, in the whole world; so it was an historical event. The work of preparing the game for broadcasting with the comments of the players was done on Saturday the 10th, from 1 p.m. to 7 p.m. After that a 50 minute radio broadcast and a 45 minute TV broadcast was ready to be aired.

In the April 1962 issue of the Danish Chess Magazine, *Skakbladet,* "Binnerup" writes that Fischer had given Larsen a good lesson in the royal game, not only during the game itself, but especially after the game. Fischer pointed out Larsen's mistakes and proven his case in the analysis.

On Sunday, the 11th of March, Fischer gave a simultaneous display in the YMCA hall in Rosenborgstreet in Cøpenhagen. Fischer played 41 players from the Cøpenhagen Chess Federation and they were very strong. It has never been customary for strong players to take part in a simultaneous exhibition, but then Fischer was no ordinary chess master, fresh from his win at the Interzonal.

Fischer was very tired at the beginning of the 6 hour contest, as can be imagined, coming straight from the Interzonal to the busy days in Cøpenhagen. He started slowly but during a coffee break, after 2.5 hours play, he regained his strength and fought hard after that. Before and during the break Fischer had many complaints. He was very angry having to play so strong an opposition in a simultaneous, and the players and the audience behaved very badly. The audience was constantly giving the players advice so Fischer commented that he was not playing 41 but 100 opponents! The players also analyzed the games by moving the pieces, which, as is known, is against the rules. The organizers tried to stop the irregularities when they became aware of them but had a hard time keeping the audience quiet. It was said that those who got the most advice from the kibitzers did not do well.

The result of this interesting event was, that Fischer won 27 games, played 7 draws and lost 7. Those who beat Fischer were: K.B. Schou, E. Poulsen, Ole Illum Truelsen, Finn Petersen, P. Nörby, Poul E. Hansen, and an Icelandic student of architecture, Sverrir Nordfjord.

Before we look at the game Fischer-Nordfjord, it is interesting to read a description of Fischer at the end of the report written by "Binnerup" in *Skakbladet:*

"Bobby Fischer is a tall lanky young man, just turned 19, who besides his natural shyness possesses a unique confidence and superiority in his manner, considering his age, when he is close to the chessboard. That he has not learnt of or seen many things in life, besides chess, does not come as a surprise. When you have in 19 years time become one of the best in the world (if not the best today) in one field you cannot demand much of him in other fields. He is a pleasant and charming guy, whom we would like to see again and we wish him the best of luck in the future, especially in the forthcoming giant struggle with the Soviet Union's five strongest grandmasters. It

is not out of the question that he will succeed in being the first in many years to wrest the world championship title from the Soviets."

Bobby Fischer-Sverrir Nordfjord
simultaneous display
Copenhagen, Denmark, March 11, 1962
KING'S INDIAN ATTACK

1.	Nf3	Nf6	
2.	g3	b6	
3.	Bg2	Bb7	
4.	0–0	e6	
5.	d3	c5	
6.	e4	d6	
7.	Nbd2	Be7	
8.	Qe2	0–0	
9.	c3	Nc6	
10.	a3!?		

This move has not often been played before or after this game. White usually plays 10. Ne1 or 10. Re1 in this position.

10.	...	Qc7

The game *Sadvakasov-Kveinys, Liepaja 2001,* continued: 10... Rc8 11. b4 Ne5 12. Bb2 Qd7 13. Ne1 Qa4 14. f4 Ng6 15. Nef3 Qc2 16. Rfb1 c4 17. Ne1 cxd3 18. Qe3 Qa4 19. c4 Rfe8 20. Qxd3 d5 21. cxd5 exd5 22. e5 Ne4 23. Rc1 Nxd2 24. Qxd2 Qd7 25. Nf3 Rc4 26. Rxc4 and Black resigned.

11.	b4	Rad8
12.	Bb2	Nd7
13.	Nc4	Rfe8
14.	b5	Nce5
15.	Ne3	d5

Better seems to be 15... Nxf3†

16. Bxf3 d5 17. exd5 Ne5 18. Bg2 exd5 19. c4 d4 20. Bxb7 Qxb7 21. Nd5 Bf8 22. Qd1 Qd7 23. f4 Ng4 24. Bc1 Qf5 25. Qf3 Nf6 26. Nxf6† Qxf6 27. Bd2 with equality.

16.	Nd2	Nf6?!

The more natural 16... dxe4 17. dxe4 (17. Nxe4 c4 18. d4 Nd3 19. f4 Bd5 20. Bc1 Nf6 21. Nxf6† Bxf6 22. Ng4 Be7 23. Ne5 Bxg2 24. Kxg2) Nf6 18. c4 Rd7 19. f4 Nd3 20. Bc3 Red8 21. Ng4 Ne8 22. Rad1 leads to a comfortable game for Black.

17.	f4	Ng6
18.	e5	Nd7
19.	d4	Ndf8

20.	a4	h6
21.	Racl	c4
22.	Qh5	Rd7

23. f5?!

Black has no counterplay so Fischer was in no hurry. He could have prepared the attack in many ways, e.g., 23. Rce1 Rdd8 24. Bc1 Qd7 25. Bh3 Bc8 26. f5 exf5 27. Nxf5 Ne6 28. Nf3 Bf8 29. Be3 a6 30. Rb1 a5 and White will double the Rooks on the f-file with an irresistible attack.

23. ...   Bg5!
24. Qe2

24. Rce1 looks better, but it leads to a difficult game for white, e.g.: 24. Rce1 Nxe5! 25. dxe5 d4 26. cxd4 Bxg2 27. Kxg2 c3 28. Ne4 cxb2 29. Nxg5 hxg5 30. fxe6 Nxe6! 31. d5 Qxe5!? 32. dxe6 Rxe6 33. Qf3 Qc3, followed by 34... b1=Q

35. Rxb1 Qxe3 etc.

24. ...   Nxe5!

This piece sacrifice is the only solution to Black's problems and a very good one too! Now White's problems on the open e-file will become too difficult to handle.

25. dxe5   Qxe5
26. Rf3?

The final mistake. 26. Rfe1 exf5 27. Ndf1 f4 28. gxf4 Qxf4 29. Rcd1 Rde7 30. Bc1 Bh4 31. Rd4 Qf6 32. Ng3 Bg5 33. Qf2 Qxf2 33. Kxf2 does not look good for White but he can fight on.

26. ...   exf5
27. Ndf1

If 27. Re1 f4 28. gxf4 Bxf4 29. Ndf1 d4 30. cxd4 Bxf3 31. Qxf3 Qg5 and White is completely lost.

27. ...	d4
28. cxd4	Bxf3
29. Qxf3	Bxe3†
30. Nxe3	Qxe3†
31. Qxe3	Rxe3
32. Rxc4	Rb3
33. Rc2	Ne6
34. d5	Nc5
35. Bd4	Ne4

and White resigned

The Fischer-Larsen rivalry

Fischer met Bent Larsen, the Danish grandmaster, for the first time at the Interzonal in Portoroz, Yugoslavia, in August of 1958. Their first encounter at the chessboard, taking place on the 16th of August, had an interesting prelude according to Ingvar Ásmundsson, one of Iceland's strongest chessplayers, who was present in Portoroz as a journalist. The following description of the events of that day appeared in his report in a Reykjavik newspaper. At breakfast, on the day of their game, Larsen said in a loud voice, that today the child would get a sound beating. He repeated this over supper obviously with the intention of Fischer hearing it and becoming nervous. Asmundsson said that Fischer, being no ordinary child, had understood that the grandmaster's statement was double-edged. With that in mind he had, in the opening of the game playing white, given Larsen the unpleasant choice between a drawn game and dangerous complications. The grandmaster did not have much of a choice after his loud "speech," but then Fischer started an irresistible attack with sacrifices, that left Larsen helpless.

Larsen was Fischer's second in the Candidates' Tournament in Yugoslavia in 1959. In an interview with the late Icelandic chess master, Freysteinn Thorbergsson, taken at the end of the tournament and published in the Reykjavik newspaper, *Morgunbladid,* Fischer said, that Larsen had been a bad second who had ridiculous ideas and who had surely learnt a lot from him during the tournament! The level-headed Fischer obviously did not like Larsen's original ideas, but the latter was, in those days, known for sometimes making unusual moves in the opening.

Fischer and Larsen were, in the sixties, the only players outside the Soviet Union who could dream of playing for the World Championship. Fischer did not play many international tournaments in those years but Larsen was very successful, probably one of the strongest tournament players of that period.

Larsen claimed first board in the match, "U.S.S.R. vs Rest of the World," in Belgrade 1970, and to everybody's amazement, Fischer accepted second board!

If you look at Fischer's and Larsen's results in the World Championship cycle, you will find that Fischer qualified for the Candidates' in 1958, had an acceptable result in the 1959 Candidates', won the 1962 Interzonal, but had a disappointing 1962 Candidates', did not play in the 1964 Interzonal, and left the 1967 Interzonal in first place in the middle of the tournament, and finally won the 1970 Interzonal.

Larsen neither made the 1959 Candidates' nor the 1962 Interzonal. He finished 1-4 in the 1964 Interzonal, reached the semi-finals in the 1965 Candidates', won the 1967 Interzonal, and again reached the semi-finals in the 1968 Candidates', where he suffered a bad loss to Spassky, and finally, was second in the 1970 Interzonal.

Their individual score in tournament games was 3½-2½, in Fischer's favor, when the clean sweep in the semi-finals at Denver took place in July of 1971, finally putting Larsen out of the race.

The Match of the Century 1972 — a Personal View

The World Championship Match 1972 was much more than a chess match. It was an international political event. The Soviet Union had dominated the chess scene after the Second World War and took great pride in that fact. The Soviets claimed that their dominance in their national sport of intelligence and logical thinking showed the superiority of the Communist System over the Capitalist System in the West, mainly in the United States of America, where chess was not popular. There was a cold war going on at that time between the two most powerful nations in the world, the super powers, The Soviet Union and The United States.

In a remote little place, Reykjavik, the capital of tiny Iceland, up in the North Atlantic, there was going to be a match for the World Chess Championship between the Soviet world champion, Boris Spassky, and the challenger, Bobby Fischer, from the USA. Fischer had almost single-handedly qualified for this match. It was, in a way, one man's fight against the whole Soviet System!

No wonder the match was called *The Match of the Century* and the world watched it with great interest.

The prelude to the match was extraordinary. The official opening took place in the absence of the challenger, who had not yet arrived in Iceland. Nobody really knew whether the match would be played.

I was a reporter for a Swiss chess magazine, *The Chess Express,* and therefore I was present when every game was being played. Looking back now, 30 years later, a few moments come to mind.

Fischer's blunder in an even endgame in Game One caused much confusion in the playing hall. The strong masters watching the game of course knew it was a bad move but they did not know what to say. The great and invincible Fischer had made the move.

Sitting in the playing hall waiting for Fischer to come to the second game was a sad affair and I really thought I was witnessing the end of Fischer's chess career.

During the fourth game I decided to sit in the playing hall and watch the players. There I witnessed something that sticks in my memory and, in my opinion, explains Fischer's strength, at least partially. I have never seen a chessplayer work so hard at the chessboard. During the whole game Fischer only rose from the table to get a glass of orange juice and, one or two short breaks. His behavior at the table was polite but very aggressive. He sat bent over the table all the time and his concentration I will never forget. You could feel that he was doing everything in his power to win the game, but the most difficult problem for Fischer's opponent was of course to cope with his strong play. It must have been a very difficult task, if not impossible, to face him at the chess table for weeks or months. Maybe this explains his success in his matches.

The 13th is the most exciting chess game I have ever watched, a great battle I will never forget. Fischer got the better of the black side of the Alekhine and won a pawn. Spassky then started to play brilliantly, adjourning the game in a complex endgame position. I remember how difficult I found it to analyze that positon. When the game continued, Spassky kept playing brilliantly and had managed to save himself, when a blunder in time trouble on move 69 threw away a well-earned draw.

During, and after the match, much of the writing and talking dwelt on Spassky's blunders and bad play and not on Fischer's performance. There was sympathy that many felt for Spassky because of Fischer's antics before the match. In every big chess event there are lots of mistakes which are inevitable in a hard fought battle, and this match was much more than a chess battle.

If you look at Fischer's results prior to the match nobody stood up to him the way Spassky did. Spassky pressed hard for wins after the disastrous games 3 through 10, and was constantly creating chances. Could anyone else have done as well as Spassky did? Fischer played very well and you can't play better than your opponent allows you to. Looking back on the match there were some very good games played, for example, 5, 6, 10, 11, 13 and 19.

I found the psychology of the match interesting. In his younger days Fischer used to say that he did not believe in psychology, but in strong moves. He had always played the same opening systems with only very few exceptions. The task of the Soviets to prepare Spassky for the opening play seemed easy.

Fischer managed to turn this disadvantage of his into an advantage. He avoided his usual opening variations as often as he could and tried to play each system only once in the match. When he repeated a variation it turned out badly for him; he was crushed in game 11. His most beloved opening systems did not score many points for him. His Sicilian Sozin turned out badly in game 4, the Sicilian Najdorf in game 15, and the Exchange Ruy Lopez in game 16 were difficult draws. Fischer stayed away from the King's Indian, and of course he did not play the Grünfeld, the cause for two previous losses to Spassky. The only successful use of a favorite system was the brilliant game 10, a Ruy Lopez.

Fischer thus managed to avoid most of Spassky's theoretical preparations and the latter did not seem to be psychologically prepared for the situation. The front page of the June 1972 issue of the the U.S. chess magazine, *Chess Life and Review,* comes to mind. There was an illustration showing Spassky and his seconds talking to the Soviet leaders, Brezhnev and Kosygin. On the table there were stacks of opening books and magazines all on the subject of King Pawn openings. The leaders asked the question: "But Boris, what if he doesn't play 1. P-K4?"

Finally a small incident cast a light on the political situation. The author of these lines was approached at the start of the match and asked if he would lend the opening books by Czech GM Ludek Pachman to Spassky's team. The books were not available in the Soviet Union because Pachman was *persona non grata* after his protests against the Soviet invasion of Czechoslovakia in 1968. The Spassky team did not want to leave anything to chance (the books were published in 1963). They returned them with thanks and an autographed Russian book when the match was over.

Fischer as Viewed by Others and Himself

It is interesting to read what other chess masters wrote about their meetings with Fischer in his best days. In this article I am going to have a look at some of the writings on Fischer in books which have not yet been published in English. Two of the authors knew Fischer very well and the third had met him and spoken to him. I will look at a few short sections from four books, two published in the Danish language and two in German, and in the final part there are a few comments from Fischer's article about himself.

Spasskij-Fischer-72
by Danish Grandmaster Bent Larsen
Publisher: The Danish Chess Federation, 1973
pages 16-17, 88

Larsen knew Fischer quite well. They probably met for the first time at the Interzonal in 1958. Larsen was Fischer's second at the 1959 Candidates tournament and they played many games.

Larsen was quite certain that Fischer was not very interested in money. He wrote that Fischer wanted more prestige for himself in the U.S.A. and for the game of chess. In Bobby's opinion money was (and probably still is) a good measure of prestige as well as being simply a means of buying prestige. To prove his point Larsen wrote that in the turmoil in the last days before the match Fischer had said to Brad Darrach, journalist for *LIFE* magazine, something like: "All this talk about money. Let's propose to Spassky to play the match completely without prize-money, just for the beauty of the game of chess."

Larsen also wrote that he was not of the opinion that Fischer's behavior before and during the match was a part of a clever plan to shake Spassky. In Larsen's opinion, the great chess strategist could be unbelievably impulsive outside the chess board, and his honesty and righteousness had often taken on unbelievable forms, both irritating and likeable. He did not find Bobby to be a bad kid, but uncalculable and sometimes unfair.

Larsen had doubts about Fischer's future. He referred to an interview, before the match in Reykjavik, with Yugoslav GM Svetozar Gligoric. Fischer said that he had spent too much time on chess and after the match he would catch up with what he had neglected in other fields.

Larsen's question was: "Will he ever defend his title?"

Today we know the answer to Larsen's question, but we don't know the reason for Fischer's decison.

Fischer's vej til VM (Fischer's road to the World Championship)
by Danish IM Jens Enevoldsen
Publisher: Bramsen & Hjort 1972
pages 187-190

Published before the Fischer-Spassky match. The late Enevoldsen was a Danish IM, for a long time the best player in his country, and in my opinion one of the best writers on the game.

Enevoldsen had some very interesting comments on Fischer, the person, the chess champion, and his chess.

He wrote that the works of great artists or geniuses never stand alone. They should always be considered in connection with the man himself. He tried to find out what kind of a person Bobby Fischer really was.

Enevoldsen wrote that Bobby was not an intellectual like all the world champions in chess had been up to that time. He had not enjoyed any school education at a higher grade. He pointed out that Fischer's lack of knowledge was not the same as Fischer's not being able to acquire knowledge. In his opinion Bobby had worked exactly like an intellectual in his studies of the game of chess.

He described Fischer as an outspoken character, difficult to please.

Fischer's behavior had sometimes been scandalous, but always with the firm conviction that he was doing the right thing.

Enevoldsen wrote that Bobby had pushed many people aside and a person like Bobby would always run into those who could not accept him and who did not like him.

He also said that Bobby was a person who was very much alive and very intense, with big shortcomings and big advantages. You could have a nice time in his company as long as you were not out to get something sensational for publication.

About Fischer's chess, Enevoldsen said that Fischer's intensive work on chess from an early age had given him great confidence, as was the case with great masters like Morphy and Capablanca. Fischer never made gross blunders. In Enevoldsen's opinion the difference lies in the fact that contrary to Morphy, he loved chess and, contrary to Capablanca, he worked energetically on chess.

Enevoldsen commented that Bobby had the quality necessary for developing a talent into genius: colossal ability to work. How he worked on his game is clearly shown in the book he had written about himself. Enevoldsen noted that Fischer had undertaken great analyses of all phases of the game, the opening, the middlegame, and the endgame. Enevoldsen found Fischer's comments on the games not without wit, but his other characteristics were in the area of lengthy analyses. Fischer had the ability to calculate variations, which is an absolute necessity for a practical chessmaster. The IM was of the opinion that strategic thoughts and evaluations were not Fischer's thing and he was far less psychologically equipped there than, for example, Spassky. Enevoldsen concluded these very interesting comments on Fischer's chess by writing that what Fischer knew, he knew to perfection.

Vlasti Hort: Begegnungen am Schachbrett-So spielen Profis
by German Grandmaster of Czech origin, Vlastimil Hort
Walter Rau Verlag, Düsseldorf, Germany, 1984
pages 33-37

Hort gave a warm description of his friend Bobby Fischer and his meetings with him. He wrote that he had known Fischer rather well in the years 1967-72 and that he had been the type of person that Fischer liked to meet. These years had been the happiest period of Fischer's life, the years he had taught the chess world to fear him.

Hort wrote that Fischer had not liked people who wanted to make use of him or saw in him a source of money. He spotted people like that from far away. As Hort had not wanted anything at all from him, their friendship had led to their analyzing chess sometimes until the early hours of the morning.

During these sessions Fischer had asked Hort's opinion on moves he himself had analyzed to perfection long ago. Hort wrote that he felt like a schoolboy asked to give an opinion. Hort declared that there was nothing Fischer valued more than a new idea or a notion.

Fischer had invited him to Amsterdam prior to his World Championship match with Spassky and there they had such a long talk in a hotel room, that they did not notice when it turned to daylight.

Hort had met Fischer for the last time (i.e., before 1984) at the tournament in San Antonio, Texas in 1972, and then Fischer was already World Champion and had only come to watch the play. Hort told how surprised he was when Fischer invited him to a gathering at the Worldwide Church of God. There he sat at Fischer's side, quiet and thoughtful, not understanding anything. He had found Mr. Armstrong's interpretation of the Bible strange in modern times. Fischer sat with a Bible in his hand with his eyes closed. Hort wrote that Fischer had been quiet that evening. Mr. Armstrong had impressed Fischer, or to put it a better way, there Hort had sensed a preacher-believer relationship, and was feeling uneasy in that situation.

A few days later Hort had dined in a Mexican restaurant together with Fischer, Gligoric and Fischer's brother-in-law. That evening Fischer was his old self again. Today Hort would give much to have the opportunity to spend another moment like that with him .

Hort also wrote about an incident in Vinkovci in 1968. He had come to the villa where Fischer was living during the tournament and found Fischer in an unusual situation. He was playing blitz with an eleven year old son of one of the organizers of the tournament. The boy was close to bursting into tears as he lost every game very quickly. Hort asked Bobby, why he did not stop playing. Bobby answered that he did not know if he should give the boy a draw in one game for educational reasons. Hort watched a few games before he left. He did not know if the boy ever got a draw. [Ed. Note: See Gufeld's story.]

Hort wrote that he agreed with the description of Fischer being a self-made man with a strong will. Further, he wrote that many journalists had tried to give the impression that Fischer had only been interested in money. Fischer's refusal to play in tournaments had often been caused by a different reason. Fischer had, for example, gone to the Olympiad in Lugano 1968 with the best intentions.

Ninety American chess fans had travelled in a chartered flight to Lugano but they never saw him play. The playing conditions were simply bad, a small playing hall, not enough space for the players, bad ventilation, and poor lighting. That was not encouraging for a good game of chess. The chess professionals today really have a lot to thank Fischer for in Hort's opinion. Compared to the fifties and the sixties (of the twentieth century) the playing conditions are much better and prize money is a lot bigger.

I am sure many professionals today are thankful to Bobby, but the sad thing is that the fruits of his fight have primarily been enjoyed by others as he left the chess stage a young man.

Fischer on Himself

Der Titelkampf Fischer-Spasskij, Reykjavik 1972
Republished in a book by Czech Grandmaster Ludek Pachman
Publisher: Walter Rau Verlag, Düsseldorf, Germany, 1972
pages 24-26

In the August 1971 issue of the Yugoslav Magazine *Start,* Fischer wrote a piece on himself. There were a few interesting comments. Fischer wrote that he would soon become World Champion and his goal would be to break Emanuel Lasker's record. Lasker had kept the world title for 27 years.

He commented on playing conditions. He said the most important was that he did not tolerate any noise, because he did not like to be disturbed at his professional work of calculating variations and making combinations. He also wrote, that his goal was to become the best on this planet in playing the wooden men. He played until the king was naked (no short draws).

Then there was a strange comment, that children who had to grow up without parents would later be like wolves. I don't know what he meant by that except maybe he was referring to fighting spirit. [Ed. Note: Others have suggested Fischer meant that children growing up without fathers must fend for themselves anyway they can, even to the point of being mean to others.]

He also said that Robert James Fischer was no computer, as some thought. He was just a man, but an extraordinary one. His world was the black and white chessboard and in his moves there was emotion or even art to be found. He was sorry for those who could not see it.

MY MEMORIES

by Bob Long, publisher

Editors, as a rule, are an unlucky lot. Many of us have access to more information about chess and "stuff" than you might imagine. For my part the amount of this information sometimes is so great that I have a difficult time locating what I need, when I need it.

Such is the situation concerning my memories of Fischer in Denver 1971 and Reykjavik 1972.

I will write what I remember that rings true, and the rest I will put on our website (when I find it), the home page of www.chessco.com, along the right hand side of your screen.

• • •

Fischer was an enigma even back then. After beating Larsen 6-0 he was relatively friendly, answered a lot of inane questions by the press (some of the worst came, unfortunately, from GM Isaac Kashdan) in a party held afterwards in the Petroleum Building in Denver, hosted by Carswell Silver. The stick-on-badge on Fischer's lapel read "Bobbie Fischer."

After the last game he was on stage analyzing with Bent Larsen, an affable and pleasant man. When Larsen was asked by an onlooker at the party why he didn't go for the draw in game six he replied, "I needed wins, not draws!" Who was to know that years later Garry Kasparov would turn a string of draws into wins against Anatoly Karpov in their first match? Anyway, Larsen wasn't the type to play like that.

I remember taking quite a few black and white pictures of various people and probably more than a few of Fischer. After awhile he became annoyed and asked me, "Do you have enough?" Surprised I said, "I'm new at this, I don't know which ones will turn out!" Many didn't look good because I shot against the window instead of from the window, but then Fischer's back would have been toward me.

I had a small publication back then called the *Chessstamps Informant* or perhaps it was *The Chess Arts*. I remember calling U.S.C.F. Executive Director Ed Edmondson about something and he invited my wife and I to the party. In spite of all of my *aggravating* pictures, I forgot to get one of myself in a photo with Fischer!

When it looked like there was a break in the postmortem of game 6, I asked Fischer to autograph my copy of *My 60 Memorable Games*. He scribbled something in it which looked like his name—always the "F" was identifiable.

Why the press and others insisted on calling him "Bobby" is not known to me as I have seen many of his autographs with the words Robert Fischer or Robert J. Fischer on them. At about age 11-12 I no longer wanted to be called "Bobby," nor my brother "Jimmy," (Robert James!) yet my father did so because it got a rise out of me.

I remember getting a picture, a rear view, of Bobby out for a stroll before the game. He walked very fast and would disappear from sight.

It was good to see him laugh. His accent seemed like a combination of Brooklyn (where he grew up) and Chicago (where he was born). He had, like most of us, certain idiosyncratic expressions. When he answered questions you could sense the honesty in his answers—answers that maybe you weren't expecting. He showed no trace of anti-anything except against the Russians (as he called the Soviets).

After all the reading I have done in preparing this book and dealing with the various contributors one thing stood out: Fischer was an amazing game player. I saw him do the Sam Loyd 15 Puzzle on Johnny Carson— greased lightning. Chess may have been his art, his work, but it was a game, and I have the feeling that he was one of the most superior game players who ever trod this earth. Whether he would have been good at poker, because of its own built-in bluff and deceit, is hard to say, but it would seem unlikely as Fischer didn't like the unknown.

I had saved about $1200 or so to go to Reykjavik in July. I had a special cachet designed for the chess event, printed on envelopes, complete with the new world chess championship stamp, and cancelled on the opening day. What a fiasco! Fischer wasn't there. These are now collectibles.

When I had taken the Loftleider flight from Kennedy in New York, I was leaving on what would have been Fischer's last flight to make it there for the big event. It was a pleasant thought, wondering if Fischer would make that late night flight but, he didn't. The Icelandic food and service on board was excellent, but didn't make up for the disappointment.

Fischer had a way of disappointing people because he was so afraid of being taken advantage of. He didn't reflect much on how things affected other people. Myself, I got to see the first game, the one he lost when he finally decided to play. The second game was a no show.

By this time citizens from the U.S. who had gone over to watch their "hero" from the States were all pretty much soured on him, including myself. Some of us took time off from work, spent all we had to get there, and we have this very bad boy behavior we wouldn't tolerate in our own children. Everyone involved with him seemed afraid of him, afraid of offending him, afraid Fischer wouldn't like them anymore.

I believe it was GM Larry Evans, Harold Schonberg *(New York Times),* and myself who got a ride to where Fischer was staying. Larry knocked on the door and Lombardy answered. Fischer was cussing out Fr. Lombardy for answering the door.

Wondering how chess was faring back home on the networks, several of us were riding in a Volkswagen through Reykjavik with GM and referee Lothar Schmid. The driver was from ABC. He told us the favorite ratings sports show on TV was *Demolition Derby.*

The hall where the event was held was big enough. So was the stage. The audience was somewhat noisy at times. They were more like onlookers than chess aficionadoes.

When Fischer "threw away" a piece in the first game due to a miscalculation, the game was eventually adjourned. One of our authors, Bragi Kristjánsson, was correct, there was tremendous confusion in the Hall. Could Fischer save himself? Was there a brilliant sacrifice involved, or what? It was an intentional move, just a miscalculation, but a lot of people had a hard time ingesting that.

Reykjavik was an interesting city. Long nights in the summer, excellent dining, many shops, roomy Mercedes' cabs, and few trees. I remember seeing a subtitled version of *M*A*S*H* at a local theater.

There was virtually no air pollution in that country and, in spite of the drizzle which fell at various times ("Gee that hardly ever happens here!"), I never caught a cold. The Dairy Queen ice cream tasted a little "off." The Icelandic girls were pretty, sometimes with a ruddy complexion. The Icelandic chess players were quite strong.

The local library was also the repository for the Willard D. Fiske chess collection. Somehow I talked them into letting me into the stacks. I was 27 at the time and feeling on top of the world.

Using limited Russian I obtained a set of photos of Boris Spassky from the Soviet Press Bureau. She was a nice lady and even though there was a picture of Lenin hanging on the wall... she gave me *all* the pictures she had! Later a French journalist saw me with these pictures in the Saga Hotel and he asked me (using a pocket dictionary) where I got them. "At the Soviet Press Bureau," I told him. I think the French have been mad at us in the United States ever since.

I asked Spassky for an autograph about the time he was going to eat—bad manners I know, I never knew if I would see him again. He was there with Ivo Nei, Efim Geller, and Nikolai Krogius. No KGB thugs were around that I "noticed," though I had seen some earlier in the week. These gentlemen made Fischer's attire look positively GQ.

Almost every day there would be something new to report in the local paper for the Reykjavik populace of about 100,000. The devilish caricatures of Spassky and Fischer became extremely popular. The original artist has died and his estate was put into the hands of some Icelandic lawyers for the widow. While we wanted to reproduce all 18 pieces of art for this book, their terms would have cost us about $9,000. Instead, they gained nothing, and neither did we.

The halibut there is fresh and easily the best in the world. However, politics is pretty much the same everywhere, including chess politics. There were a number of conferences, some of them lame, some informative. During these "meetings" one could come in contact with all kinds of chess persona such as Al Horowitz, Max Euwe, Svetozar Gligoric, Dmitrije Bjelica, many grandmasters, and just fine people such as Bill Wheeler, Texas State Champion.

Books were everywhere on Fischer and chess. Banners in businesses, souvenirs, and such let the visitors know, as if they didn't already, that there was a big deal in town, just like the old time circus.

I understand that when Fischer started winning the sentiments reversed themselves back to the Commie Killer. All in all, I was glad I went.

Fischer never followed through on his promises; you can't lose if you don't play. He would've tamed Karpov or Kasparov if anyone could have gotten him to the table. Instead, he became a legend.

Be sure to check out more details at www.chessco.com for our Icelandic adventures.

Bibliography

Bobby Fischer heute, Das Genie zwischen Wunder und Wahnsinn by Yves
    Kraushaar, usus (1977)
Bobby Fischer: Instructive Games of Chess by Eduard Gufeld, Fizkultura i
    sport (1991)
Bobby Fischer vs. The Rest of the World by Brad Darrach, Stein & Day (1974)
Der Titelkampf Fischer-Spasskij, Reykjavik 1972 by Ludek Pachman, Walter
    Rau Verlag (1972)
Fischer's vej til VM by Jens Enevoldsen, Bramsen & Hjort (1972)
Grandmasters in Profile by Dmitrije Bjelica, NIP (1973)
Morgunbladid, Icelandic newspapers
My 60 Memorable Games by Bobby Fischer (1969)
Russians vs. Fischer by D. Plisetsky & S. Voronkov, Chess World (1994)
Schachphänomen Bobby Fischer by Alexander Pasternjak, Olms (1991)
Skakbladet, Danish Chess Magazines
Spasskij-Fischer 72 by Ludek Pachman, Danish Chess Federation (1973)
Vlasti Hort: Begegnungen am Schachbrett-So spielen Profis by Vlastimil Hort,
    Walter Rau Verlag (1984)
Worldwide Church of God website

Special Thanks

I wish all of the following pages of photographs were first rate, but they aren't: scratches, black and white film, amateurism, etc. all add a bit of nostalgia rather than absolute professionalism. Yet many, for the record, are quite interesting and offer glimpses which would otherwise not be seen and avoid what we have seen many times before.

In 1956 Fischer was just 13, playing Sam Skaroff, U.S. Amateur. Do you recognize the clock (Solara) which was used years later in the 1969 match between Spassky and Petrosian? Photo courtesy of John Donaldson.

The beginning of the game before the famous adjourned draw at the Varna 1962 Olympiade in Bulgaria. In the foreground Boris Spassky is starting his brilliant game (one of the best in olympics' history) with GM Larry Evans. Photo courtesy of Arinbjörn Gudmundsson.

Fischer conducted several simul tours including the big one in 1964. This is Leicester, Mass. Note the undraped tables. Fischer went on to demand the respect chess deserved. Photo by Glen Wheeler, courtesy of John Donaldson.

Larsen and Fischer postmorteming Game 6. In the background is Mrs. Larsen and E. Klein, the arbiter. © Bob Long.

The lobby at Temple Buell College in Denver, with its fantastic mural. Mrs. Mercedes Long (seated) has a copy of Bobby Fischer's *My 60 Memorable Games* autogaphed by none other than Robert Fischer

Although often portrayed as hostile to the press, after the 6-0 whitewash against Bent Larsen, Fischer listened and answered all questions. He holds a copy of the Denver newspaper which covered the match. © Bob Long.

**Fischer's
Rating
History**

1726
2231
2298
2362
2420
2626
2636
2640
2641
2659
2660
2675
2713
2687
2659
2664
2674
2685
2734
2706
2708
2713
2748
2758
2762
2741
2754
2739
2745
2755
2748
2762
2755
2771
2801
2825
2824
2810

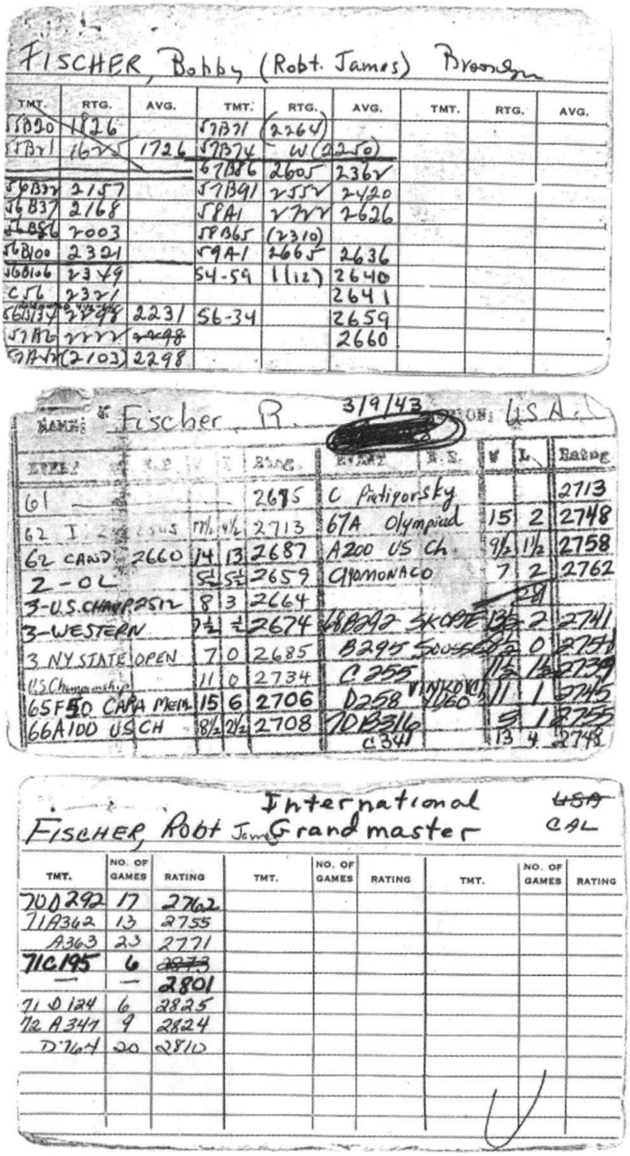

**Fischer's USCF rating card. Courtesy U.S.C.F.
Assistant Exec. Director Eric Johnson.**

Game 3 through the "Back Room" monitor. Photo courtesy Icelandic Chess Federation.

Euwe acts as though he is looking at a tote board for Fischer's "expected" arrival. Arbiter Lother Schmid seems stunned. 1972, Reykjavik. © Bob Long.

Fischer talking with Icelandic Chess President Gudmundur Thorarinsson, who wrote a chapter for this book. Thorarinsson's frustration with Fischer's demands are well-chronicled in Darrach's book *Bobby Fischer Vs. The Rest of The World*. In many instances Thorarinsson stood firm and was one of the few to show courage in his dealings with Fischer. See his new look at the 2002 Commemorative Conference in Reykjavik on page 187. Photo courtesy of the ICF.

There were journalists from everywhere. Above left is I.A. Horowitz (NY Times), and GM Miguel Najdorf. Photo courtesy of the ICF.

Inspecting the view are, from L to R: B.H. Wood, publisher of *Chess*, and whose 64th birthday was celebrated in Reykjavik. Next is Chester Fox (owner of the camera), and to the right is Dmitrije Bjelica. Photo courtesy ICF.

From L to R: Milunka Lazarevic, the nicest looking person in Reykjavik, Frank Brady (former editor of the much-admired *Chess World*), and GM Bent Larsen listening to IM Jens Enevoldsen, also from Denmark. Photo courtesy ICF.

GM Bent Larsen (Denmark) has almost everyone's attention in the analysis room. It wasn't uncommon for Icelanders to be able to also read/speak Danish, English, or German… as the bookstores testified. Photo courtesy ICF.

What a difference 30 years makes! ICCF-IM Bragi Kristjánssen, our Icelandic researcher. Chess player then, lawyer now. Currently team captain of the Icelandic Men's National team. Photos courtesy of the ICF.

30th anniversary of the 1972 world championship match in Reykjavik, Iceland; ceremonies in the Culture House. Icelandic President Olafur Ragnar Grimsson related that 2 years earlier he received a phone call from Fischer, who at that time was in Japan, about the 1972 event—which he had read about on the internet.

L to R: Boris Spassky, Lothar Schmid (arbiter), Gudmundur Thorarinsson (ICF president in 1972). ©2002 Dadi Jonsson.

30th anniversary of the 1972 Fischer-Spassky match. Reykjavik, Iceland ceremonies at the exhibition, Icelandic Chess Heritage and The Match of the Century. Spassky retests one of the boards used in the famous match using a Jaques set. Looks like one of our "Gambit" wooden clocks to his left. He faced an unknown opponent. Besides Lothar Schmid, and Gudmundur Thorarinsson (former president of the 1971 ICF), GM Helgi Ólafsson was in charge of the panel discussion. Ólafsson is one of the current contributors to "Skak," the Icelandic chess publication.

©2002 Dadi Jonsson.

Index

Colophon

Bobby Fischer: From Chess Genius to Legend was typeset in Adobe's Times. Diagrams were made using TPI's *C.R. Horowitz®*. Text was set 12/14.

The Team
Cover Design: Ken Prestley, Blue Sky Communications
Compiler/Editor: Bob Long
Layout/Design: Bob Long
Proofers: Mark Donlan, Nate Long, Bob Long, John Donaldson
Indexing: Bob Long
Original Translation: Marina Sonkina

Contributors: Andy Ansel, John Donaldson, Davi Jonsson, Bragi Kristjánsson, Bob Long, Eric Tangborn

Special Permissions: Manfred Olms (Olms Publishing). Some photos were obtained by Bragi Kristjánsson through the Icelandic Chess Federation archives—we thank them both.

Back Cover Photo: Taken by the publisher after Game 1 was concluded. Picture taking was not allowed, but at the end of the game I noticed several flashes going off from the audience, and I took a couple with a Nikon which had been tucked under my raincoat. It is blurry and aging, but as there were so few color pictures taken at this event, we wanted to give you a glimpse of what it looked like. Rob Long was responsible for what little retouch could be made. There is also a color photo on the cover of Purdy's book on the match.

Karpov · Kasparov · Smyslov · Euwe · Petrosian · Tal · Botvinnik · Lasker · Capablanca · Fischer · Alekhine · Spassky · Steinitz

CHESS' THINKERS

copyright © 1999 Thinkers' Press, Inc./ Bass Long. All rights reserved.

A nice full color print is available of the above world chess champions, painted by Los Angeles artist Rob Long. Size is more than twice what you see above. Suitable for framing. $9.95 + $5.95 S&H. Available from:

CHESSCO
1101 W. 4th St.
Davenport, IA 52802
Toll Free: 1-800-397-7117
Visa and MasterCard accepted.

Would you like a copy of our current chess catalog? If so, please send $3.00 and one will be rushed to you. Please allow 7-10 business days.

Our website in known world wide by:

www.chessco.com